Awaken
your Inner Faerie
in 30 Days

First published by Sixth Books, 2013
Sixth Books is an imprint of John Hunt Publishing Ltd., Laurel House, Station Approach,
Alresford, Hants, SO24 9JH, UK
office1@jhpbooks.net
www.johnhuntpublishing.com
www.6th-books.com

For distributor details and how to order please visit the 'Ordering' section on our website.

ISBN: 978 1 78099 716 2

A CIP catalogue record for this book is available from the British Library.

Design: Lee Nash

Printed and bound by CPI Group (UK) Ltd, Croydon, CR0 4YY

We operate a distinctive and ethical publishing philosophy in all
areas of our business, from our global network of authors to
production and worldwide distribution.

CONTENTS

For
Every woman

With
Big Cosmic Cuddles and thanks to

Anntina Quinn – for being a brilliant friend throughout this book's birthing process.

Tess Clarke – for showing me how brave a person can be without even knowing it, how passion is next to goddessliness and for tirelessly and emphatically telling me I should write, write, write!

Emmy Morrisroe – for bringing me back to life.

Lennie Varvarides of MSFT productions who took a chance on my first play and who told me that 'nothing happens until you push'.

Introduction

So you want to awaken your inner faerie in 30 days. Well, firstly, do you have the nerve? The passion? The burning desire? I think you do, but do you?

Secondly, do you know what you are unleashing? Your inner faerie is not present in faerie lore or story books. She will be totally and magnificently unique. She is that bright, glittery, passionate, energetic, positive, enthusiastic side of you – the side that often lies hidden or neglected for fear of ridicule, failure, criticism, or lack of love. Who knows what she will do once liberated? She may stir up your relationships, change your career direction, buy a motorbike and go joyriding across the American plains ...

Do you still want to awaken her? Good, then let's begin.

Why I wrote this book

There are two reasons I wrote this book. The first is that I know you are a creative being. You are not just a passive observer of your world; you are a pulsing magnetic powerhouse of creative energy! You just have not had the pleasure of meeting that side of yourself yet, if ever. Once you meet her, your life will become a magical series of events and enjoyable synchronicities – I want that for you. Secondly, I believe you deserve a wonderful loving insightful relationship with yourself – once achieved you will live with less fear and more love, which is good for everyone! Relationships like this require courage; it takes a brave woman to live from her creative faerie core. In essence, I want you to connect with your magnificent inner faerie-self and infuse your life with her passion. Why? Because it would make me smile and I like smiling. Really, it is that simple.

Oh, and I also love writing. I believe in the power of words – I have watched them change people's perceptions of themselves and their world for ten years now. They still continue to change mine. Words vibrate like guitar strings, or an old banjo, depending on what music you're playing to the universe. They have the power to heal or harm, create or destroy, confuse or enlighten. Words are magic.

My passion is sharing with you what I know to be true for me and others – no matter how dark it gets, you can always turn towards the sun. I want you to finish this book and have found a way to really like yourself, to really enjoy living within your own skin, being awake and walking your life with pride and self-belief.

"It must be really nice to like yourself" someone said to me at a workshop. A statement draped in such sadness and certain desire, as if she thought it had always been this way for me – it hasn't.

My own story starts back in inner-city Manchester. It rains a lot in Manchester. It is an old industrial city, filled with rows and rows of terraced houses. We were poor and often hungry. Now I can hear some people saying that poverty in the Western world doesn't leave people hungry, especially in the early '80s. But all you're really saying is you haven't encountered families with multi-faceted problems. Once you have, you'll accept that real poverty still exists. It can be overcome, but it is there. In my time as a family support worker I have seen families with shoeless children living in homes infested with rats. But this is not my time to offer you a desperate sob story, there are enough of them about and I am not a victim of my circumstances, not even when they have been dire. However, I have lived a very real life, in a very real world.

By the time I was 20, I had experienced bullying, rape, addiction, homelessness and teenage motherhood. At 21 I attempted suicide. Now, at time of writing I am 33. I'm a writer, healer and most importantly happy. I run workshops on fairy magic, healing and writing. I am alive, happy, and energised by the thought of being inside every day. The full account of my recovery is in the biography at the end of this book. After you embark on this programme and reach my story you will see that many of the questions and hurdles you had to overcome, I too encountered. I am not unique. What is most profoundly experienced by one is often experienced by all. You are not alone on this journey.

I chose the faeries to help me write this book as they are easily accessible and hold the right symbolic representation – to be honest, they can be pushy eager energies and I often feel they chose me. They are going to help you rescript yourself and your life. They will encourage you to giggle, to dance, sing and give thanks. They are here to tell you that it doesn't matter if you live on streets of grey, by a motorway or in a high-rise flat, for beneath the asphalt, the earth breathes in unison with you and your heart beat. Always. They help you remember that everything beneath you, above you, around you and within you is made of the same stuff. The stuff that makes stars, the stuff that holds the universe together. You are currently connected to every time, every universal space and hidden sphere of imagining, yes you … no matter who you are, no matter if you live in downtown New York or in the Himalayas. All space is sacred. All is part of you and us. You are always whole, even when you feel like a fragment. Remember that no matter how your story began, you get to decide the end. Even stories set in stone are eroded by the power of nature.

Why now?

What a dark age we live in – 24 hour news, war, poverty, recession, global warming, beasts roaming Bodmin … the list is endless. If light workers are here to usher in a new dawn of spiritual enlightenment they better hurry up, but their first challenge is to stop watching 24 hour news. Fixating on how dark it is never turned on a light. It's the equivalent of:

'I'm hungry'

'Here's a sandwich'

'Yes, but I'm hungry'

'Eat the sandwich then'

'I would, but I'm hungry'

Darkness is around and you will encounter it, but you will conquer it too. How? You will eat the sandwich – or rather dive into this book. Turning on lights takes a little training and discipline. No wait, don't close the book! It can be fun; it should be fun, in fact *only* fun can turn the lights on!

This is why I will not be dwelling on the darkness in this book. It is a purposeful choice. There is a lot of dwelling going on, a lot of climbing into swamps to prove they drown you. The modern fixation on what I call 'the Fear' is not helpful. If darkness is mentioned within this book, there will be a counterweight, method, or pathway back to the truth – Light conquers all. Darkness – fear, sadness, rage, hate, disgust are all *only* vibrational frequencies. I say only because vibrations can be changed. Yours is already different from the moment you decided to pick up this book. By the end your vibration will have shifted even further.

Wibbly wobbly vibrations

Everything in existence vibrates. Nothing is stable, resting or kicking back and taking a break. Everything is humming whirring and dancing at differing speeds – frequencies. Your frequency gives you the illusion of separation from everything around you i.e. there appears to be big gaps between you and say the wall, the tree outside, the birds flying overhead, the sun ... and so on. You are not separate. At a quantum level you are connected. To quote a bellbottomed hippy I once knew (he knows who he is) 'we're all one baby'.

Thoughts and feelings are vibrations too; they reverberate

through us, helping us to feel empowered or powerless. Why am I telling you this? Because they also communicate with the universe in ways we are yet to fully understand but science is just starting to unveil. Your vibration, the union of emotion and thought into your healing heart centre pumps out your secret messages to the universe every second of every day. This book will change that union, make it more harmonious and beneficial. It will subtly bypass your left-brain through creative activity to rewire your sacred mind-heart connection. We won't spend long discussing this here so bear with me. I just want to show you enough to realise how amazing you, yes you, really are! You are a seriously magical bubbly cauldron of creative possibility.

Research by The Institute of Heart Math (titled: Local and Non local Effects of Coherent Heart Frequencies on Conformational Changes of DNA: phew what a mouth-full) demonstrates this powerful, baffling universal connection beautifully.

The researchers placed twenty-eight samples of magical remarkable human DNA in separate containers and gave them to twenty-eight magical remarkable trained researchers. Trained in what? Trained in how to feel, yes feel.

So we have twenty-eight research scientists with twenty-eight samples of human DNA. What did they do? Well, they had to direct their feelings towards their DNA sample. When the researchers felt love, kindness, nurturing, gratitude etc, the DNA strands unwound. Yes, they relaxed. When less helpful emotions were directed the DNA contracted. It tightened. Wow eh? We are not only connected. We are able to influence that connection. Become an artist with your emotions and you will woo the universal vibration. This book will show you how.

Hang on! It is not a question of positive versus negative.

Energy is given meaning via differentiation and preference. Understanding your emotions vibrationally means you become less inclined to hold onto them. If one good thing comes from this book, it will be that you become less enthusiastic when infusing 'the Fear' with more meaning and weight than joy and happiness.

'But I am sad'

'But he did do this'

'But I don't have that'

'But there are people who suffer, die, hurt others ...'

There is. You're right. You are very observant.

But how does it feel to be right?

Seriously, sit a minute. Close your eyes. How does it feel being right? Do you feel strong? Do you feel energetic? Do you feel love? Enough love to share and extend it to all who live without it? Do you feel powerful, as if you have many choices before you?

How does it feel to be right?

Got it?

Whatever you are feeling right now is your vibration. You are pumping that frequency out into the universe by being 'right'. You are not righting any wrongs. You are not helping the needy or expanding your experience. You are contracting into fear. From a place of fear you can't change anything. You can't help anyone. You can't expect to look into the dark and see light. If you concentrate on what is lacking you will just feel lack ~ and the universe will mirror your expectations.

I'm interested in you moving forward and sometimes being right doesn't help the journey. You need to be open to the idea that you are wrong, wrong, wrong about yourself and the world! Sometimes protecting your right to feel bad only gives you permission to be stuck, standstill, or manically chase your tail for fifty years – all of which you are free to do. This book is about looking beyond right towards the possibility of a life filled with conscious happiness, lightness and creative passion – because believe it or not, you have a right to let go. You have a right to move on from any and all the injustices you have experienced; you have a right to decide what life you want next. This book is your spiritual sandwich, here to satisfy your spiritual hunger.

Where do the faeries fit in?

Faeries are closely connected to mother earth. They want to help you re-script your inner beliefs so you can connect you to your effervescent, childish, silly and playful-self. They like to empower, play, create and move fast! They will connect you to the light within you! Once you are consciously connected to this inner truth you will shine so brightly the darkness around you is transformed and transcended ... believe me, you will never miss the old you. Yes, I can read your mind; you may fear your life will become dull, fluffy and sugary once you embrace your inner faerie. But, I assure you nothing could be further from the truth, your life is about to become radical, magical and infused with passion purpose and excitement. You are about to become whole. And from this place of wholeness your new universe can be formed, shaped and coloured with the fluorescent paints of your choosing.

Yes, you guessed it. This book is fierce in its attempt to reconnect you to joy. Silliness, laughter, smiling and playful mocking is encouraged because you need to laugh more. Everyone needs to laugh more. Life is a game, play it well. The aim of my words is to change your vibration ~ you will vibrate in happy and pump happy out into the universe, into your life and into other people's lives. Your inner giggling revolution will have beautiful healing far-reaching consequences.

Naive I'm not, (well not all the time) and I know at times you may feel resistant to such radical change in how you perceive yourself and your world. Such blocks may include:

Guilt – manifesting in statements such as:

'What would people think of me if I did that? They'd think I'm
   a selfish old cow that's what'

(Add your own here)

Anger – erupting in statements such as:

'Be positive? My house has been repossessed, I've no job, no qualifications, no hope of getting any and you're telling me to be positive!'

(Add your own here)

Sadness – thinking in terms of:

'What's the point? The world is filled with so many beautiful things I'll never experience; the world isn't made for people like me and the more I think about it the more depressed I feel'.

(Add your own here)

Doubt – manifesting in self-talk justifiers such as:

'Yeah, yeah, being happy, whatever. They just want me to buy more books don't they eh? Like anyone gives a damn how I feel'.

(Add your own here)

I'm not here to mock you. In fact these statements are all mine from my old personal development diary. They are simply used to show that we all think the same toxic stories from time to time. And now it's time to re-write. The old stories are not serving you; they are boring out-of-date re-runs of the same old sitcom. You need a new story. You are safe at all times. I am not here to hurt you. I am only here to tell you one thing. Lightness is your birth-right.

Say it to yourself.

Lightness is my birth-right.

I'm only here to show you ways you can claim this. Whether you do or not is up to you. It doesn't make you right or wrong and I only have one word of warning. I will be relentless, absolutely fearless and in your face when it comes to telling you that you are brilliant, amazing and truly worthy of a wonderful life! I will be forceful in pushing my opinion that you deserve an awesome, loving, creative and forgiving relationship with yourself! You do deserve it, you can have it, it is waiting, it is close, it is within you, reach out and take it! You have the power to make it a reality!

Are you ready?

Day One

Discover your Faerie Clan

The whole point of this 30 day programme is to make you more comfortable with your wild self. When we think of faeries we think of this wild child-like spirit which resides within us. That's who we want to prod awake. This essence is pure creative force. It is raw, magnetic and radical. You will feel like starting projects, changing direction and throwing away your telly in favour of a paint-brush.

Faerie lore is infused within all of us. Its colourful metaphor and meanings shape and form our ideas about magic today. Even in contemporary society, you just need to look at the amount of fairy-tales, songs, festivals, magazines and films we have starring our winged counterparts to see that faeries are still relevant in our daily lives. We love our winged friends and yet there are many theories on what they are! For me they are elemental energies vibrating at high speed which can be worked with in co-operation with the faerie to bring about healing and/or change.

When working with women, I see that faerie energy is the fastest way to rekindle their passion for life. Faerie likes to use story, metaphor, magic, acting, music and feasting to help people rediscover their lost selves or uncover pieces yet to be seen. They work in unpredictable and irrational ways at times and therefore make excellent teachers and they are eager to lead you to their classroom.

To me the universe is one great big metaphysical ecosystem, some parts seen and felt while others lie unseen and undetected. The ecosystem wants to thrive, grow and expand. This forward motion, this expansion, this ceaseless growth, is reflected in all living things. Humans tend only to see their own small part.

However we have also become far too reliant on our physical senses to tell us the whole story, a bit like looking through a keyhole and expecting to see the whole house. We don't see moving beyond innocence, naivety and youthfulness as progression, we see it as decline. We look at what we lose instead of what we gain. Why? Because we are unaware of the role we play in the universal ecosystem. Therefore we fear our own death; we see loss rather than a natural cycle that expands the evolution of the whole universal ecosystem. The universe will just keep on expanding and as we are one with her – we'll just keep going. Yes, you are right. There will be a time when none of this 'matters' – quite literally.

So now you know what I'm going to say next, right? Of course you do. You and faerie are the same thing. They are nature, you are nature. They are the creative spark in you and the creative spark in the universe. They make you fertile with ideas, creativity and positivity. You can see them as pretty-faced winged beings if you like, or lights, or music, or metaphorical psychological parables … believe what you like, so long as it is helpful and enables you to become the best possible version of you.

Am I pecking your head?

'What you on about?' said a young woman on a workshop in Manchester 'yer peckin' me head.' Everyone appreciated her honesty, including me. Look, right now, you don't need to worry about the big scheme. You don't even need to understand it. No one does anyway; otherwise it would all be different. The universe reflects our focus like a photon under a microscope reflects the observer's intention. You only need to self-focus. We get out what we put in, so to speak, and I'm here to help you put in love so you get love out. The rest will then fall into place with no effort whatsoever. Okay? Cool.

Faerie clan fun

A secret of mine is that I have been talking to faeries my entire life. I noticed how they have different feels and personalities. When I started my healing career these personalities became clans. Each clan had a healing sigil and an empowerment sigil, animal totems and more which they lent me to help others. By incorporating this knowledge into my work it was very easy to see people as already healed and whole – it works wonders.

The clans are made up of archetypal energies. An archetype is a collection of character traits that accumulate to create a powerful personality symbol e.g. the magician tarot card. Simply looking at this card means you could list numerous meanings belonging to it. Okay okay, some of you are shouting 'stop compartmentalising! Everything is One! You just said we are all the same consciousness experiencing itself subjectively', and like I've said before, I agree. I'm happy you recognise this already, but not everyone does or can stay in that enlightenment long enough to make significant changes to their lives. Please, recognise how lucky you are and foster patience for those who want to experience this realisation. Oh and P.S: yes, we are all one. The universe is one large spider's-web, glistening in its silvery infiniteness, so please ... stop shouting at yourself hoping someone else will hear.

Back to the point. Faerie clan work is a fun way of looking at how you are vibrating right now and what may be out of balance. It is the process of understanding your self-story/script so you can creatively re-write a new more beneficial self-story with the faeries' help. Don't worry; it's going to be lots of fun! It's not like school, you won't be writing essays, but you will be playing games, drawing silly pictures and doodling 'I love me' on your exercise book. Okay, so maybe a bit like school, but you have my permission to hitch up your skirt and take off your tie. First off you are going to find out which faerie clan you belong to.

This quiz is not an exact science (it's not a science at all) but it does provide insights into who you are and how to proceed with the 30 day programme. Knowing your clan helps me provide you with a more personalised programme, perhaps the most individual way I can do this without seeing you as one of my clients. So when you have your pencil case ready we'll start the quiz.

Who are you? The Caterpillar ~ Alice in Wonderland

Answer the following questions as truthfully as possible and then complete the initiation ritual to meet your clan queen. She will be your guide and confidante during your 30 day programme.

Faerie clan quiz!

What attracts you to working with faeries?
   a. It's a new idea and I'm always exploring new concepts.
   b. I love them! They always look so lovely and colourful.
   c. Energetic little things aren't they; I want a bit of that!
   d. I hope it helps me heal myself and others.
   e. They sound like fun – plus I hope it gives me an excuse to wear bells and dance about a bit.
   f. I'm hoping it offers me the chance to understand myself and others better.
   g. They appeal to the part of me that feels out of sync with the world.

What type of films do you watch?
   a. Oh, something Sci-Fi, the Matrix, Star Wars, maybe Blade Runner even.
   b. Oh something foreign and arty; Amelie or Pan's labyrinth. Failing that 'It's a Wonderful Life'. James Stewart is a god.
   c. Modern classics such as Thelma and Louise, Erin Brockovich or The Shawshank Redemption.

d. It may seem a little odd, but I do like a good Disney movie. The Lion King, the little mermaid ... in fact, anything in which the bad guys get their come-uppance.

e. Oooh anything with people lost in the woods, or stuck in haunted houses. Boo!

f. Any and all films ~ I love stories of all kinds.

g. Lord of the Rings, Narnia, the Golden Compass, I really enjoy a good fantasy.

What is/would be your dream occupation?

a. Psychologist/scientist/new technologist.

b. Painter/photographer/filmmaker.

c. Activist/environmentalist/campaigner.

d. Medical/healer/educator.

e. Musician/singer/composer.

f. Journalist/novelist/scriptwriter.

g. Actor/performer/comedian.

What's your ideal holiday destination?

a. Oooh, visiting NASA, no wait, the moon!

b. Anywhere with trees, open space and beautiful landscapes.

c. Somewhere hot, with a beach and tequila, mmm Mexico.

d. A yoga retreat to clear my soul, aura and chakras.

e. Glasto! Mud, music, messy hair, oh yeah bring it on!

f. Paris, bookshops, coffee, a large notebook for all my inspired ideas. Bliss.

g. Cannes film festival ~ then somewhere quiet to recover, maybe a hideout in the Swiss mountains with lots of fresh air and hot chocolate.

What do you want from a friendship?

a. Someone who wants to talk about my projects, we'll get round to talking about theirs eventually but firstly ...

b. Someone who doesn't mind me snaffling their gorgeous

clothes before we go out to nice places and meet interesting people.

c. Someone who will be with me through thick and thin ... and be willing to give me an alibi if I accidentally kill someone.

d. Friendships are about giving not taking, so I don't really want anything.

e. Anyone who doesn't talk half way through a song ~ seriously though, that's really annoying.

f. A person willing to explore their experience with me, so we can witness each other's journey through life.

g. Someone not too demanding, who can give me space and when they are around can talk sense, not gossip.

What do you want from a lover?

a. Intelligence, a beautiful mind is hot.

b. Fit body, no seriously I'm not joking, I have to find him attractive or it's not going to work.

c. Honesty. I'd much prefer to know the truth than have anything hidden.

d. Mysteriousness, there's nothing sexier than a tall, dark, handsome brooding stranger

e. The willingness to talk about emotions ~ I need to feel supported.

f. An interesting conversationalist, an evening spent chatting is worth any amount of foreplay.

g. Faithfulness ~ I can give or take anything so long as I know he only has eyes for me.

If you had to choose one gift for your child/ren what would it be?

a. An inquiring mind. Curiosity never steered anyone wrong, unless they were a cat.

b. Creativity, it's the ability to look at life sideways and still see it as something beautiful.

c. I want them to stand up for themselves. Take no B.S kids.

d. To be happy. If you are happy everything else solves itself.

e. Popularity. Charm and charisma make the world go round. I mean, look at Boris Johnson; he's made a full career out of it!

f. To be fulfilled. To know their purpose and fulfil it daily.

g. Success ~ to have the strength, perseverance and willpower to set a goal and then reach it.

How would you describe yourself?

a. Innovative, I'm a spiritual entrepreneur.

b. Artistic, I'm imaginative and see beauty in unusual places.

c. Protective, I'm the lioness of the family, (no, not big and hairy) I mean I'm fierce when it comes to keeping those I love safe and happy.

d. Loving. I try very hard to be loving in my thoughts and actions to all living things (sometimes even with inanimate objects, but I'm weaning myself off that type of behaviour).

e. Connected, I'm grounded while still being aware and connected to my spiritual-self and the world around me.

f. Wise. I have learnt my lessons well and now try to live by what I have learnt.

g. Misunderstood, I often feel people misread what I am about and sometimes judge me harshly without trying to get to know me.

If you could play any instrument what would it be?

a. The decks and I often think I could be an MC too.

b. Piano, it makes such a sweet sound!

c. Drums. They are the heartbeat of all music.

d. Harp, it's so angelic and healing.

e. Voice, singing is free and fun to do, especially in the supermarket.

f. Guitar, I love their definite, assertive, deep sounds.

g. Violin, they have emotional range, sounding light-hearted one minute or melancholy the next.

Which natural phenomenon best describes you?
   a. Shooting star – bright, unusual and gassy (maybe not gassy).
   b. Northern lights – rare colourful and strange (strange can be good).
   c. Tornado – fast, chaotic and destructive (only if pushed, I'm not crazy).
   d. Whirlpool – deep, powerful and impressive (impressive? I meant to say intense).
   e. Lightning storm – electrifying. Enough said.
   f. Earthquake – authoritative, earth shattering, commanding (but never lasting for long).
   g. Mirage – not quite what people think they see (not that I'm duplicitous, I'm just different).

Where would you love to live?
   a. Eco-village with all the mod cons, I want to save the environment but still have internet access.
   b. In the countryside ~ somewhere I can watch the sun setting.
   c. A villa in Italy, or Spain, or Greece, overlooking a beach filled with hunnies.
   d. Anywhere by the seaside! Well maybe not Blackpool, but you know what I mean, the coast. Maybe a brooding coastline in Scotland somewhere.
   e. Anywhere I can wake up and hear the birds singing, but not a zoo obviously.
   f. I like the idea of city living, somewhere I can visit museums, libraries, theatres and yes, spend afternoons people watching.
   g. Somewhere breath-taking ~ like Iceland, the Canadian Rockies, or Niagara falls.

What do you find most challenging in life?

a. Social situations ~ people are so strange.

b. Dealing with negative people, moaners make me moan.

c. All the pain and injustice I see happening to people, the world can be so unfair.

d. People not accepting my love and help, I just want people to be happy.

e. Staying grounded, I just love daydreaming too much!

f. Seeing the bigger picture yet feeling powerless to change anything.

g. Finding true love, everything seems so disposable and superficial these days.

It's party time, where can you be found?

a. At home. I don't do parties.

b. Strutting my new outfit and red hot shoes ~ can't dance in them, but I have perfected a mean swagger to the bar.

c. Debating politics with anyone who'll listen!

d. Making sure everyone is included, fed and watered and yes, I know it's not my party but someone's got to do it.

e. Showing off my moves, oh yea, on the dance floor, watch me! Over here!

f. Watching, talking and after a few I'll probably dance ~ badly.

g. On the periphery looking for a conversation to join, before boredom sees me home for an early night.

What's your favourite way of getting about?

a. Electric car. It is a perfect piece of engineering

b. Quite like the bus, I can sketch unsuspecting passengers.

c. Motorbike ~ I need to get places fast.

d. A people carrier, so no one feels left out.

e. I like to ride my bicycle, I like to ride my bike.

f. Train, if I can. There's something special about a train that connects me to the past while I move into the future ... oh my god, where's my notebook I need to write that down!

g. My own car, sitting next to strangers makes me uncomfortable.

If you were to open a shop what would you sell?

a. Gadgets and helpful inventions for the home.

b. Art work, my own, maybe street art, in fact anything colourful and cool, umm maybe shoes.

c. Coffee, people need energy to deal with the day.

d. Crystals ~ our little healing helper friends need homes.

e. Music ~ then I could blast out my favourite tracks all day long.

f. Books ~ old and new, all styles and genres.

g. DVDs of all the latest movies, apart from the latest Johnny Depp ones, they stink. Old Depp is best.

You are preparing your favourite meal, what is it?

a. Pot noodle, I'm too busy with important things to cook.

b. Oooh something Mediterranean, reds and greens and tastes galore!

c. Something light I can eat while on the move, sushi, sandwich, salad, food generally beginning with S.

d. A good old honest roast like my mum used to make.

e. Hummus with ... well anything really.

f. Good comfort food, pasta's good.

g. People still cook? I'll order in if that's okay thanks.

What's your most positive trait?

a. I understand energy, matter and find physics strangely fascinating ~ are these positive traits?

b. I always see the good in situations and people.

c. I'm loyal; sometimes it has been taken advantage of though.

d. I'm very caring and always want the best for people.

e. I'm the life and soul of the party, I make people smile.

f. I'm a good listener, can solve a problem and offer sound advice.

g. I'm self-aware and take ownership of my own emotions and behaviour.

What's your most prized possession?

a. My mind, now pass me the Ginko and crossword I've got to keep the grey matter limber!

b. All my trinkets are beautiful and prized, oh I can't choose, don't make me please.

c. I prize my ethics and ideals above all else.

d. My family and friends are the best thing I own.

e. My iPod. Fact.

f. My notebooks, they have all my creations inside.

g. My lover, he is my world.

If you had the power to bestow any gift on yourself what would it be?

a. Ability to freeze time, that way I wouldn't always be up against the clock all the time.

b. Beauty, nothing is grander nor more powerful.

c. Invincibility, failing that mediumship so I could amass an army of ghosts to kick butt.

d. Healing powers, then I'd heal the world one person at a time.

e. Precognitive ability, so I could see next week's lotto numbers.

f. Time travel, I could go back in time and discover how things really were before the winners wrote the history books.

g. Manifestation abilities, I wish I could just think of what I want and have it appear in front of me.

If someone wrote your biography what kind of book would it be?

a. A book about my career and amazing discoveries that benefited all humanity.
b. Gold gilt, red velvet, succulent and gorgeous, oh what kind of book? Hopefully not a horror.
c. An inspiring read for anyone trying to overcome adversity against all the odds.
d. A book for anyone needing comfort and reassurance, maybe a self-help book on healing.
e. A manual on how to be awesome.
f. An insightful paperback that the reader can carry anywhere.
g. I think pictures paint a thousand words so it would mainly be photos and meaningful quotes.

Mostly A's
Samiel of the Stars

You resonate with the Samiel of the stars – the cosmic faeries. Flitting from star to star, planet to planet, the Samiel are interdimensional. They wear crowns made of constellations; have brilliant transparent wings and eyes of shocking ice blue. The Samiel are masters of sacred geometry. They are the galactic scientists always discovering new ways of doing things and coming up with new ideas and concepts. They have flexible nimble minds making those who resonate with them top entrepreneurs, innovators and scientists. They are also master mathematicians, playing with abstract notions with ease and grace and find new technology as blissful as Buddha finds mudras. Possibilities are seen where others only see problems and their idealism infuses all with the glittering promise of miraculous change. Being an interstellar faerie, Samiels sometimes misinterpret people's needs, not being earth bound can cause empathy malfunctions. The Samiel's totem is the ladybird, who shows up to teach you how to ground your ideas into reality and how to connect with others in meaningful loving ways. Resonating with Samiel can be tricky in a world of seemingly pointless social structures and institutions so using the crystal Celestite will balance your energy as its high vibration is infused with divine energy promoting auric healing, empathy and peace of mind.

Mostly B's
Frey of the Wild Places

The Frey reside in forests and woodlands. Their kin have a keen understanding of nature, her cycles and their place within the whole scheme. Natural beauty radiates from the Frey clan, they have a sparkle in their eye which comes from their keen willingness to seek out all things pretty and surround themselves with them. Often wilful, often alert, often seeking some colourful trinket the Frey make excellent photographers and filmmakers as they understand beauty, have an instinctive understanding of symbology and an uncanny ability to read body language. The Frey's soul is filled with neon lights, but if not able to express their artistic temperament, they soon stop seeing beauty every-where. Instead the world becomes a cruel and dark place. Freys should never lose hope. Use Orange Calcite to get your creative juices flowing, energize your sexuality and alleviate depression. The Frey's clan totem is a magpie, finding their feathers is the Frey telling you to keep your faith in all forms of beauty, your own and other peoples'. At night the Frey send Moths to help us find the light in the dark, which is never far away even in the dead of night.

Mostly C's
Duna of the Desert Sand

The Duna are the warrior clan. They are strong, athletic and striking in their beauty. They have a hot temperament when witnessing injustice, cruelty or discrimination. Natural protectors they will fight on behalf of anyone less fortunate, not stopping until they get their desired result. Fair, just and honest the Duna make excellent activists, advocates, charity workers and we certainly need more entering politics! They are courageous on behalf of others but sometimes forget to stand up for themselves as they believe they are stronger than others. If this goes on too long they can start to suffer from displaced anger outbursts and victim mentality. Use Amethyst to neutralise anger, fear and grief. The Duna's clan totem is the Wasp, who buzzes up to help you go your own way rather than following the current trend or crowd. Wasp also shows us how to move into solitude when we feel angry, frustrated or irritable.

Mostly D's
Mimi of the Sea

Mimi of the Sea are guardians of the earth's waters. Mimis encourage us to dive deep into our unconscious to discover the key to our hidden motivations and desires, their brightly coloured butterfly wings remind us that we'll emerge from the depths able to fly again. Empathy, unconditional love and maternal energy make Mimis natural healers. People who resonate with Mimi need to remember to heal themselves before others, eventually you will become an excellent healer, therapist, or medical professional. To start your healing journey try the crystal Rose quartz for its calming, peaceful and loving energy. It releases the stress and pressure on the heart chakra and instils unconditional self-love, promoting deep inner peace, forgiveness and self-esteem. Mimi's clan totem is the butterfly to remind us that transitioning and change is up to the individual, we can help, but we cannot enlighten those who enjoy playing in the dark.

Mostly E's
Silim of the River Bank

The Silim clan are nature's musicians they gather at river banks listening to the gloop of feeding fishes, harmonies of humming reeds and the occasional squawk of an angry duck. In fact the Silim could easily become transfixed by their own heartbeat! Those who resonate have an understanding of nature's own rhythm and have a personal connection to the earth which transcends language. The Silim understand that everyone's song is valid and amazing and so make excellent sound healers, singers and composers. Their ability to read the pauses, silences and intonation in other people's speech patterns can seem magical ~ and is. Silim also have an ability to transcend ego and surrender to the present, they can also alter states of consciousness at will, however if taught to doubt their natural abilities or without a healthy practice of consciousness altering meditation the Silim can develop an inability to voice their opinions, creeping apathy, loss of vitality, shyness and fear of people. Use purple fluorite to aid meditation, bring about inner peace and calm. The Silim's totem is the bee which shows us how to work as part of a group. Bee arrives to tell us to be focused, committed and disciplined to achieve our dreams.

Mostly F's
Omil of the Tree Roots
The Omil clan live in hollows and tree roots; they dress in gossamer and have pointed wing tips to punch holes in lies and corruption. They are compulsive truth tellers. They also like to sing into spiders' webs to watch the universe wobble. They understand words change worlds. The Omil understand language as frequency which makes them excellent writers, journalists and storytellers. They have an otherworldly ability to see emotional power games being played and how they will pan out. They communicate in words easily and can often cook up an interesting anecdote or two, or three hundred. Sadly if found in an environment where secrecy is the norm, or self-deceit encouraged, the Omils can feel themselves going round the bend.

They end up looking at the world with despair and disgust; sometimes retreating into solitude and sleep, pottering, generally grumping about and sleeping some more. Use the crystal chrysocolla as it speeds up the metabolism, aids communication and promotes tranquil energy by eliminating the guilt associated with truth seeing and saying. The Omil's totem is the spider who shows up to say 'Hey! You can change this! Weave some magic words together and let the manifestation unfurl ... '

Mostly G's
Jimji of the Mountain Top

Jimji are statuesque beauties. They reside on snow-capped mountain ranges; their brilliant green eyes are distant and powerful. Those who resonate with the Jimji can carry an unintentionally intimidating presence. Often giving the appearance of a still lake; barely a ripple of movement on their serene faces, but beneath a wealth of emotion stirs. However, they don't often feel the urge to communicate their experience with others. They are self-contained, emotionally restrained and puzzling to others. Jimjis are connected to themselves like no other faerie clan, making them brilliant actors and performers of all kinds. Their strong physical presence has the ability to inspire others to create or perform feats they would never normally consider. The Jimji often confuse this influencing ability as coming solely from their physical beauty and can end up living in fear of aging or being found imperfect. This can encourage feelings of worthlessness and a worthless Jimji is prone to jealousy, possessiveness, and self-destruction. Try citrine which is crammed with sun energy to attract wealth, prosperity and happiness. It increases confidence, raises self-esteem, enhances sexual power and promotes personal power too! Dragonfly is your totem as it reminds you reality is just an illusion so lighten up and enjoy the ride.

So there you are. You have taken your first step; you have found your faerie clan. Now are you ready to connect to your clan queen? The one who will be your guide for the next 30 days? The following exercise will connect you with your elemental mother, ready or not, here she comes ...

Day Two

Meeting your Faerie Clan Queen

Here it is! Your initiation into your faerie clan. It takes the form of a visualisation journey. A journey is the shamanic term for inner consultation. The process of travelling to the inner worlds to create outer changes, it is a way of communicating with your spirit self and retrieving information. You need only journey within to find all the answers to your questions. Be prepared, however, for whatever insights you may receive. Remember that every aspect of you is trying to protect and love you if we are prepared to look beyond appearance and behaviour to find the divinity.

According to shamanic cosmology, there are three inner realms of consciousness: the Upper, Middle, and Lower Worlds, these worlds are inherent in the collective unconscious, are woven into the matrix of the psyche and can be accessed if you know how. Some use ritualised drumming, ingesting psychotropic herbs, controlled breathing or active meditation such as journeying.

You can read this to yourself in stages, closing your eyes where indicated. Or you can record yourself saying the words and play them back to yourself. Failing that get someone you love and trust to talk you through it.

Once you have met your clan queen, write down whatever you noticed about her; remember she will be your ally for future exercises over the next 30 days.

Excited? I am ...

Entering the kingdom journey
Time: dusk, preferably during a waning moon when the inner

world takes precedence over the outer.

Space: candle lit, gentle incense, comfortably heated.

Breath: 4x4 breathing. (Breathe in for a count of four, hold for four, breathe out to a count of four, repeat four times or until you become still and peaceful.)

Close your eyes when you feel ready. See yourself surrounded by a brilliant golden light. See how the light glistens and sparkles like gold dust vapour; as you breathe in you inhale this magic, gold, sparkling air, as you breathe out, you exhale all your worries, concerns, fears and anxieties. You are free to let your mind and body be absorbed and neutralised by the golden light. You are free. You are safe. You feel lighter, and lighter. Breathe in, breathe out. Notice how calm you are in this space.

You can see a large ornate tree. Ribbons of all colours and trinkets of all sizes and shapes hang from its branches; it is a much loved tree. You feel generations of love radiate from its bark and from its roots. In its branches you notice a bird, who notices you. You welcome each other. You walk towards the tree and as you do a door appears. You approach the door feeling excited by what lies beyond. You walk through the door and into a brilliant bright white light, you are overcome by a feeling of tranquil peace, the brilliant white light moves around you like mist, it is soothing and soft against your skin, the mist finally clears and you find yourself standing at the foot of a tall, impressive castle.

You notice a small hole in the castle wall. Intrigued you peek inside and observe some beautiful winding stairs. Notice how eager you are to climb them. You ascend the stairs and come to a door. You notice and remember the number on the door. You enjoy breathing so deeply, so calmly. You open the door and step inside the room beyond. A familiar scent greets you. There is shelf after shelf of fresh and dried herbs, potions and glittering crystals. You notice their magnificent colours, their geometric shapes and unusual yet familiar names. You touch and smell all that interests you, noting how they make you feel. Eventually you notice another door. You approach feeling eager and excited by what could lie beyond. You feel you are on the brink of a life changing moment. You walk through the door. Inside is a huge decorative library. There are books of every size and description lining the shelves, comfy seats and large wooden tables. You are filled with a sense of awe. Inspecting the shelves, you take off books that interest you and leaf through their pages. You choose a book and sit comfortably in one of the chairs; you are surprised by how fast and easily you absorb the book's message. You hear a gentle and pleasant sound which you soon recognise as music; you close the book and stand up. Walking towards the melody you find it leads you to another door. Again, you are excited and enter feeling child-like with curiosity. On the other side is a large courtroom, there is a large empty golden throne. On either side you notice musicians are playing instruments. There is the wonderful evocative scent of sandalwood. You approach the throne feeling compelled to kneel down. You close your eyes, breathing comfortably and peacefully. You feel a warm friendly loving glow flood your body, filling you with love, deep unconditional love. You open your eyes and look up at the throne. Seated there is a beautiful, magnificent, faerie woman. Your faerie clan queen. She greets you. You observe the shape of her face, the brilliance of her glinting sparkling eyes. The way her wings catch the light. Your faerie clan queen leans towards you, takes one of your hands and places a gift onto your palm. She kisses your forehead and you realise it is now time to leave, she leads you from the courtroom towards a small door, it opens for you as you approach, stepping through and finding yourself back where you began by the wonderful magical well-loved old tree. You look at the gift in your hand feeling calm, reassured and very very loved.

You wiggle your toes and stretch your fingers and start to feel yourself resurfacing and re-entering your current life, still peaceful but refreshed, filled with clarity and much love. You open your eyes slowly and enjoy being back in your room, in your life and within yourself. Remember at all times you are very very loved.

Jot down as many details as you can remember of the journey. This is the beginning of your awakening.

Day Three

Party Planning

Give yourself a massive pat on the back, your journey to the inner faerie kingdom has begun. What do you mean you feel no different? That's because you are at the beginning and beginnings are places filled with promise and sometimes trepidation … and of course excitement. Permanent lasting change will occur with each step towards your goal of living more creatively, authentically and magically. Research suggests it takes 30 days to learn a new way of thinking or master a new skill, daily repetition and dedication is key. Sounds too big? Don't worry, I will be breaking your activities into 10 day segments so they are easier to chew and won't break your teeth.

Today's activity is really good fun. It is to plan your faerie birthday party. You have 30 days until you are reborn! Let's make it a celebration to remember. Grab a pen and paper and let your imagination run riot.

Faerie parties are not about the people you invite, the decorations you have or the music filling the space. They are about you celebrating you and your life! You can be alone in a basement flat or on a mountain top beneath the stars, your party is not a status symbol, it is a celebration.

Fae friend experience

When Alex gave me her book I was like what you on? Me and me son Danny were dossing in a smelly bed and breakfast in Ancoats. We'd been living there since I left his dad, it was an abusive relationship and I was struggling with depression. Danny was four and loved the idea of a faerie party. But we had nothing, seriously nothing. We had one room, a quilt, and lived on pot noodles, hugs and just pulled ourselves from one day to the next. The ideas in the book pulled me and Danny together, by the time the party came, I was feeling strong. We made faerie cakes, a den with our quilt and told stories. We cried together that night. That night, something changed. It's still one of my best memories.

~ Angela, 27

Make your party as special as you can. Make it about your achievements, your journey and your future. Write down the sights, sounds, scents and tastes you want to fill your party time with. You are giving yourself a well-deserved gift.

Day Four

Creating a Faerie Journal

For the next 30 days you will be documenting your journey. Whether morning or night, a faerie journal is the perfect place to record your thoughts, feelings and magical experiences, this is important for a few reasons.

1. You will be creating a private place to examine who you are and who you want to be.
2. You will be cultivating a safe place to ask questions and look for answers.
3. You will be giving yourself space to focus your thoughts and intentions.
4. You can look back on your entries and see your progress.
5. You can log all your interesting journeys, meditations, dreams and synchronicities.

The journal can be as fancy or as plain as you like – it's yours, do what you will with it! Just update it daily. Ritualising change, to begin with, helps create new neural pathways in the brain and we all love a new neural! Plus, once we start to look and notice the magic of our world, the messages that arrive appear clearer and this clarity will flood our lives enabling us to focus on what is important to us.

Day Five

Create a Sacred Place

A sacred place is a space of empowerment. Fill it with items you find empowering to such an extent that you feel better simply by being within the environment. Your space is a sensory heaven in your household. Fill it with objects, scents, colours, and textures you find luxurious, beautiful and powerful. If you have the absence of one sense for example sight, cram your space with material you like to touch. As a minimum for all I recommend your favourite incense, a feather and a candle. Each day you are going to honour yourself in this space, so make it reflective of you, the parts of you that you really like and approve of showing to the world.

This may sound like more trouble than it's worth, especially if, like me, you have a small home. But I assure you it will reap golden results. Even if you have to move your sacred space from one place to another, due to overcrowding, it's still worth doing. For instance, some people have a room. They fill it with stuff that creates a magical mind-set, whereas others will have a portable space, like a bag of trinkets and ornate items that they can move from room to room if the house gets too busy and therefore can set up a sacred place on the hoof.

Ideas for a sacred place setting:

a tree grove
a table
the bath
a box (portable)
a bookshelf
a windowsill

What you keep in or on your sacred place is up to you. Many magical people will tell you of all the paraphernalia you should own, but be wary, try not to approach anything from a point of need or approval. This is about what provokes your inner faerie to buzz to the surface, some like shiny things others like leaves and clay. You are unique, treat yourself as such. Approach this activity from a place of want, inspiration, desire, passion or love. Cram your sacred place with things you genuinely hold sacred, otherwise it holds no energy and isn't fit for purpose. This sacred place is meant to change your vibration by the mere act of sitting in its vicinity, so choose pictures, figurines, photos and well anything else which fills you with hope, happiness and wellbeing simply by being near it. You are aiming to smile, come to life with energy, not fall into a coma. Choose well. Here is when knowing yourself comes in handy. I have known people with amazing sacred places that evoke no feeling in the owner; they have been created to inspire a feeling of awe in other observers. Please remember that how you feel is more important, how you feel is how you vibrate so, if you love Dr Who, put figures of Dr Who on your sacred space, if you love dandelions paint the place dandy, if you love firemen who have accidentally and inexplicably lost the top half of their uniforms ... you get the picture? Feel the difference. Surround yourself with what makes you smile.

No matter how small, your sacred place is a powerful symbol in your life. It is your heart. You should keep your faerie-journal there as your faerie work should be a great source of joy.

Day Six

Energising Ritual

Bold vitality is the name of today's game. Today you will be shown how to zap your home, your sacred place and yourself with an energising ritual to keep everything bursting with fresh bouncy energy. You can aim to do this daily, preferably in the morning; don't worry, it will only take seconds.

You need:
Any citrus/bergamot oil or a few drops of lemon juice mixed with water in an old spray bottle.

What to do

Stand inside your sacred place and imagine a small golden circle at your heart, imagine this golden heart circle growing larger and larger with each out breath until the sparkling golden colour is filling your entire body. Keep breathing the golden light out into your room and into your entire house. When you feel yourself and your home is filled with this tingling zappy energy call on your faerie clan queen.

State your clan queen's name .... thank you for filling me, my home and my sacred place with your giddy brilliant playful energy. I know I am safe on all levels of time and space and that all my intentions and dreams are unfolding before me. I thank you for walking with me as I discover all I need to know.

Take your citrus spray and spruce up the energy of your home with each squirt!

Day Seven

Cleansing Ritual

Wow your first week is over! By now your daily routine will have changed significantly, daily energising, journaling and now cleansing. Energy cleansing is so important especially for sensitive souls or empaths. Empaths have a very difficult time keeping their energy fresh as they are like sponges for other people's thoughts and feelings. With practice you will be able to cleanse and align your energy by shifting your thoughts and feelings to more positive ones, for now you will be ritualising the process to give yourself a firm understanding of what it feels like to be within your own energetic self.

Ingredients:
Sea salt or lavender oil.
A bath or shower.

What to do

Follow this process at the end of each day. Fill a bath and add 1-2 drops of lavender oil and a sprinkle of salt. Call on your faerie clan queen and state:

Your clan queen's name ……….. thank you for cleansing and aligning my energy, fill this water with your healing love to fill in any holes in my aura and remove any energies that are not mine or that don't benefit my higher purpose.

Imagine the bath tub filling with pure magical love.
Climb into the bath and visualise yourself inside a clear bubble. Fill this bubble with brilliant white light. Remember to

breathe comfortably and evenly. Relax and take gentle note of how your energy feels when fresh and cleansed. Soon you will be able to evoke this alignment by will alone. If you have a shower, simply adapt the ritual by making a sea salt body scrub. Mix the salt in a bowl with 1-2 drops of lavender oil and gently rub away the day's tensions while using the visualisations above. The Silim like to show up during this ritual, so make a note of any light anomalies or faerie silliness occurring!

Day Eight

Honouring Yourself

You must do this next exercise every morning until your faerie birthday. It is non-negotiable. You are making a pledge to yourself. You are going to start worshipping yourself as the embodiment of the feminine aspect of your faerie clan. A faerie goddess so to speak. This is very difficult for many women. We have been living in toxic times, encouraged to carry some pretty horrible views about ourselves and other women. Undoing that damage is key to reaching your faerie self. Faerie women like other women. Liking other women requires liking yourself first. As what we say about others often reveals more about how we view our own shadow selves, becoming fully whole requires loving ourselves completely ~ darkness and all. Looking at how we judge and disapprove of other women can reveal how we judge and disapprove of ourselves. These judgements create a powerful shadow self who lurks in the lower worlds of the psyche sabotaging our best efforts in an attempt to be given love and approval. Delving into our judgements can help us love our shadow and become a whole person.

But firstly, use this space here to make a list of all the things you value in yourself.

We will use your list to make a prayer to the self.

I am ...

So you have a list of seemingly innocent words. Some may not feel that authentic or true and perhaps you even struggled to find more characteristics than the usual, I am kind, I am caring or I am loving. That is ok. Good going. Here's what we are going to do next.

Put your three top traits into a short prayer like this:

I thank myself for being ...

Today my ... will shine out into the world.

I am safe to be ...

(To see my own self-prayer go to 'About Me'.)

Now, every morning until your faerie birthday you are going to get a mirror, yes you are, and you are going to look deep into your own gorgeous eyes and repeat your prayer 3 times. Note how you feel. Try to smile while praying; you are doing a wonderful thing. But don't worry, if you can't, 'The Good Morning Dance' will crack you up for sure.

Day Nine

The Good Morning Dance

The Silim are so excited about this chapter, anything musical gets them grabbing their fiddles and drums. The Jimji are gearing up too, they don't mind a bit of bopping. In fact you can call on either clan to help you with this task; they are energetic and eager to help. Now I'm not asking you to become a bopping Tasmanian devil, but I'm asking you to explore the concept of cleansing the self through movement. Seriously, shaking your money maker first thing in the morning can enliven your whole day! It is also a great way to put your ego in its place. Look, I know you're thinking, 'it takes three coffees before I can remember how to dress myself in the morning' but you are soon to be proved wrong. After dancing every morning for the next 21 days (yes you read that right) you will be renewed, energised and invigorated. Any self-consciousness will have been discoed out of you and coffee will be a thing of the past!

I'm not stupid, I'm may be odd, but I'm not daft. I don't expect you to be boogying on down for half an hour, in fact ten minutes will be a big ask for most of you, so I suggest you pick one song, your favourite one, or a blinding stupid one, (see list below for suggestions) and dance until it ends, every morning, whether you like it or not.

The idea is to connect you with how you feel and demonstrate how quickly this state can be altered. You may feel grumpy to begin with and 'I hate my life' type of dancing might result – that's ok because by the end you will feel different. This difference may only be slight, such as an 'I hate Alex Clarke' type of dancing, but it is a change and this shows just how much control we have over changing how we feel. You may feel embarrassed and stupid. Good. It's okay to feel stupid and it's even better to feel embarrassed. Embarrassment is conquered by enduring its clammy strangle hold, once our ego has been dressed down, toughened up in the right places we are left more resilient ~ we are liberated and free to succeed. Faeries are clowns and you will need to get used to feeling daft. Silliness is a good friend.

You will eventually move into your own way of dancing and may even end up loving shaking it up in the morning! For those who are really confused right now (Samiel Clan I'm looking at you) here is a walk-through method of the Good Morning dance:

Pick your favourite piece of music.
Shake your booty.
Yep, it really is that simple.

Selection of good morning bop music:

Purple People Eater – Sheb Wooley
Ocky tocky unga – The Wiggles
Queen – Big bottomed girls
Blondie – Rapture
Bob Marley – This is love
T-Rex – We love to boogie
The Bangles – Walk like an Egyptian
The Bees – Chicken payback
Green Day – Dominated Love Slave
Wizo – The Count
Bonzo Dog Do Dah Band – Mr Slater's Parrot

Don't forget to tell us all your favourite music for the Good Morning Dance on Facebook or better still you could always share a video clip of yourself in mid bop!

Day Ten

Attitude of Gratitude

All the effort you have been putting in to this change is commendable, well done! So far you are journaling, cleansing, energising and dancing daily! How are you feeling?

Now we are going to add the practice of daily gratitude. Gratitude can be combined easily in the evening with your cleansing ritual and when performed from a place of humble appreciation it can change your life.

The Duna Clan tend to find gratitude practice the most difficult to assimilate into their faerie work. You are natural warriors and activists. The world needs you to keep this fire, but gratitude will not put the flame out. Gratitude keeps your inner furnace hot and your heart open. Nothing will dampen a Duna's spirit more than constant focus on what they want to change. Give yourself a break and focus on what's going well.

Look at the positive. Magnify it! Simply list three things that have gone really well that day, or in your life generally. This can be hard sometimes. I have experienced some very dark times. Times when even breathing felt like a curse – in those times we can be grateful too. Yes, we can be grateful that this too shall pass. Seconds passing changes everything. Time is relentless in moving us forward. The only certainty is change. Be grateful for change.

Initially you may feel resistance to gratitude practice. A lot of people feel they have little to be grateful for and although I do not want not to minimise your pain or suffering, I want to tell you to take momentary relief from it. Gratitude if practiced carefully and from a place of nurture and love can enable healing and spark change. I'm yet to meet an adult who wasn't told as a child to be grateful as a form of punishment for wanting more or something different. There is absolutely nothing wrong with wanting more. If our ancestors had been satisfied with what was available then, we wouldn't have houses. Indeed as a species it could be said we are hot-wired for progress. Yet, wanting more doesn't mean we have to declare the present as awful or discount the beauty of the journey. The journey is the point after all. Therefore, gratitude in this sense is simply appreciation. Appreciating now does not block ambition, it enables it, because appreciation energises you and your world – by looking at your life from a power perspective you have a larger ability to choose.

Moving into gratitude

Sit in your sacred place. Focus on your breathing. Become aware of how you feel, breathe this feeling out. Remember a time when you felt great peace or safety and breathe that feeling in. Think of your chosen gratitude events, or people you feel fill you with great appreciation. Enjoy the feeling as you breathe for as long as you wish. Smile. Life is wonderful, generous and working for you.

Record your brilliant discoveries in your journal with a little glitter and a smiley face.

Day Eleven

Meditation not Medication

It's time to introduce the idea of meditation. Don't panic! I have taught meditation to loads of people who believed it was beyond them or they were too stressed, busy, imaginative, sleepy, or bored to experience the effects. Seriously, meditation is not beyond anyone. All you are doing is altering your brain waves and you do that all day long without even realising. All meditation does is give you the power to do it at will and with beneficial intention. Contemplative neuroscientists have found that even in novice meditators concentration, empathy, and positive emotions are magnified within days.

By introducing stillness to your day you will improve your health instantly. Research suggests that those who meditate have lower blood pressure and greater wellbeing. Sounds good eh? Yep, it is. Right, firstly let's clear up some common misconceptions regarding meditation.

Q. Er, don't I have to like, stop thinking?
A. Good luck, that's never going to happen, if you are waiting for that then all I can say is don't hold your breath. The trick is to let go of the thought, without adding to or exploring its meaning, just let it go. Think it, place no emphasis on it, then watch it float away. If it helps, imagine yourself as a third person observing your thoughts and feelings.
Q. If I'm not relaxed, I'm not meditating, right?
A. Not exactly, meditation comes in many shapes and forms from Buddhists picturing themselves dead in order to release themselves from the fear of death, to elaborate

story type walkthrough meditations. Meditation is not relaxation.

Our original state is bliss. If you remembered your true power you would return to this bliss. Bliss is your core. It is present within you right now. Here is a simple meditation to get you started.

Bliss meditation

Sit in a quiet spot, breathe comfortably and become aware of how good it feels to take in each breath. If your mind drifts, don't chase the thought, just remember to come back to your breathing. Once you feel calm and peaceful try the following while breathing blissfully:

Inhale strength, exhale fear.
Inhale love, exhale fear.
Inhale wisdom, exhale fear.
Inhale tranquillity, exhale fear.
Inhale peace, exhale fear.

Move your awareness into your chest, to your heart, picture a small white light glowing and pulsating centrally in your chest. Be non-judgemental with your feelings. Don't attach a good or bad diagnosis on how your heart feels, just observe the sensations.

Close your eyes.

Breathe love into your heart and see your heart shine bright with brilliant white light.

Breathe out and push the light through your whole body.

Continue 7 times (Or longer if you desire).

Open your eyes.

For each faerie clan there tends to be a tool that can aid meditation.

Samiel Clan

You may benefit from using Mudras (yogic hand positions) try the Bear Grip said to stimulate the heart and empathy will help you connect safely and authentically with others. Place the back of your right hand to your chest. Chest (thumb points down). Then your left fingers grip your right fingers in a type of hand shake. Hold while breathing.

Frey Clan

You may benefit from using mandalas which are beautiful shapes representing wholeness, the cosmos and your own sub-conscious landscape (and we just thought they were pretty patterns!). Try making your own by drawing a 10-inch diameter circle, now take a ruler and make a dot in the centre. From the dot, measure 1cm out and put another dot and so on … once you have your dots, draw circles inside the circles. Now relax and decorate your circles in colours that make you smile. When you have finished your creation you are ready to sit with it in meditation. Contemplate your choices …

Duna Clan

Candle meditation is practiced by gazing at a candle flame, simple eh. Well not exactly. This meditation is challenging. Gazing softly into a flame may sound easy but your eyes will water and want to blink. However, for Dunas it's perfect for burning back anger and building healthy warrior energy as the conflict and challenge is within you, not with those outside you.

Mimi Clan

Imagination is key here! I want you to imagine you are a cone of incense. Imagine you are burning slowly away, giving off the most wonderful scent. As you burn you are giving away joy, love and abundance to the universe. Just marvel at how much your light is giving to the world!

Silim Clan

Chanting equals neurosis dissolving, compassion building, immunity boosting and voice cleansing! Plus it doesn't cost a penny. Pick one word which encompasses what you are seeking (this will change over your journey so don't sweat getting it right, there is no right) for example 'love' repeat this singular word in a loop, dragging the sound out as much as you can to fill the full breath before looping back with another breath to start again. Enjoy!

Omil Clan

Just like the Duna, the Omil clan are best with a sensory challenge. This challenge is coupled with an intuitive task. Sit quietly. Breathe calmly. Feel which part of your body has a message for you. Place your right hand, with left on top, onto this area and breathe love into your body with each out breath. Continue until the sensory conversation ends.

Jimji Clan

This is a visualisation meditation just for you Jimji. Get comfy. Close your eyes and breathe long steady breaths until you forget about your breathing. Visualise a daisy. A small, delicate, white daisy growing from the moss at the root of a large tree. Do this meditation every day until you finish this book. Make sure you record your impressions too!

These meditations can be done daily alongside your gratitude practice in the evening. You will find the two practices will begin to merge over the next few days. Don't be alarmed, this is the point. You will end up with your very own unique way of meditating and reaching your bliss centre. Experiment! When you have a discovery come and share it with us in the Faerie Ring on Facebook.

Day Twelve

Help! I'm Freaking Out!

Let's check in. How are feeling? Many of you will be feeling fantastic! Way hey! Keep going honey-pies; you are giving yourselves the biggest gift you can - love, happiness and peace of mind!

Experience tells me some of you will be feeling a bit freaked out. Why? Well not everyone has lived the same life, if like me you have had a turbulent past, are a curious questioner, in possession of a massive imagination you will have undoubtedly encountered fear over the past seven days. You have made huge changes to how you live day to day, it will have thrown up old emotions and issues - perhaps new ones that you didn't even know were lurking!

This is why I set up the faerie ring groups. They are spiritual witnessing groups that offer safe supportive spaces to explore experiences of becoming whole people. I urge you to join our online network via Facebook to meet other likeminded people.

Yet before you rush off, I want to assure you that the fearful disturbance you feel is natural and normal. It will pass. You are starting to look at yourself in a more positive way and if your past has been steeped in religion, abuse, or gender oppression of any kind you will be feeling resistance. You will want liberation but fear what it will mean in your wider life and relationships. Perhaps, like a moth to a flame, you are feeling a bit singed right now. Don't be frightened. You will be loved as a whole person. You are worthy of a better life and that is all you are moving towards. Practice the following ritual in times of uncertainty and fear.

The sacred seal

While standing, breathe in to a count of four, hold for four, exhale to a count of four. Repeat 4 times. Call on your faerie clan queen. Feel her presence. Ask her to step into you. Feel her power radiate through you. Take your right hand and place it on your brow and say:

'I am protected by the truth.'
Then place your hand on your heart and say, 'I am protected by all powerful love.'
Place your hand on your solar plexus and say, 'I am protected by my connection to the truth of all powerful love.'
Lift your hands outward and say, 'I am protected on all levels of time and space.'

After a few times performing this affirmation you will get the same effect by simply touching your brow, heart, hips, and space around you. If you are encountering resistance within other people, I urge you to try the following method to protect yourself as you grow in personal power and happiness.

There are probably others who are not suffering from fear but impatience. You may be asking, how is this making me more creative? To you I say, be patient and persistent. Creativity is a way of being; you have been gently tapping your wild mind to awaken its potential. We have some creative activities coming over the next few days and then you will pick, if you wish, a creative project to pursue. All good things arrive when they are meant to arrive.

Day Thirteen

Forgiveness is the Best Medicine

Every power princess in the making requires a strong ability to forgive herself and the flaws in others. It frees the heart and mind to pursue other activities and dreams. We live in a very unforgiving time and perfection is pushed upon us from every angle; a lovely warm remedy to a seemingly cold pushy world is forgiveness.

I forgive me ritual

Sit in your sacred place. Breathe deeply and calmly. Close your eyes. Call on your Faerie queen to help you if you desire. State out loud:

'It is safe for my unforgiven self to appear to me now.'

Visualise yourself sat in front of yourself. Notice how your other self looks. Is it different to you? How old are they? Do you see the root of their fear? See how it reaches out from them and into you. Place your hands on this root and say:

'For all and everything real or perceived I forgive you.'

Notice the root melt and disappear in your hands.

Notice how they lean forward and open their hands, inside are two glowing golden lights, take the lights and breathe them into your heart. Sit for a few moments, breathing deeply and calmly as you assimilate this power. Open your eyes.

Please take notes on how you feel during this activity as you may surprise yourself with your findings. You can also adapt the ritual to forgive others too by changing who you visualise. The more you can let go and progress forward the lighter you will feel, but it should always be your choice when to let go. If you are experiencing difficult or stubborn emotions check out the section entitled 'Difficult Emotions' for an exercise designed to bring relief.

Day Fourteen

Meet your Clan Totem

Today I am exceedingly excited for I get to share my favourite aspect of faerie work with you. Clan totems! I love working with the faerie friends, animal spirits, tree spirits and crystals rock my world. Your clan totem is the power symbol of your faerie family. They hold hidden qualities that we can attune to and learn from. Native American Indians saw these totems as spirit allies, whereas modern shamans see them more like psycho-spiritual symbols that either reflect our own innate qualities, or parts of ourselves that we need to heal or accept so we can understand our selves at a deeper level.

Journeying is different to meditation. It is more active than passive and is believed in some cultures to be the soul literally journeying to the spirit world to gleam information and power for its return. Whatever you believe, it is a process rich in symbology and personal imagery that can aid your personal and or spiritual development. Your clan will dictate which totem you are seeking on your journey. (see below) It is also beneficial to play some gentle drumming or meditation music to aid the process, check out www.shamanicdrumming.com for free music downloads!

Totem symbolism

Samiel's ladybird

Ladybird's power is unconditional love; she shows us how to be open to all forms of love, understand love on all levels and communicate our love for others without the need to possess them. Ladybird also awakens us to the possibility of luck and abundance on all levels. She can invigorate our self-belief and trust in others as well as deepening our connection in existing relationships.

Frey's moth

Moth is the guide through inner intuitive worlds – she is tutor on all things psychic. Moth is guided by the moon and will show you how to attune to your own lunar cycles. Moth's power is sexual allure; she'll show you how to be a more passionate sexual partner, enabling you to learn the art of surrender and higher sexual union. Moth is a remarkable sexual healer and will impart wisdom regarding trust, attraction and fidelity.

Duna's wasp

Wasp is the symbol of evolution, natural order and progression. She'll show you how to usher in new beginnings and take control of your life. Wasp's power is in social connections. She tells us to speak our truth, connect authentically with others, and assert our boundaries. She shows us how to be independent without becoming isolated, reminding us that socialising is as important as working hard.

Mimi's butterfly

Butterfly is the symbol of transformation; she'll show you how to accept any big changes that occur in your life with grace and peace. She understands transitions and life-death cycles telling us that there is beauty and significance in the transient moments if we can learn to let them go. She helps us practice non-attachment and how to live in the present.

Silim's bee

In ancient Egypt the bee was sacred to mother goddess Neit and was said to bring prosperity, good fortune and poetry. Bee brings inspiration, invokes sunny feelings and motivates us to follow our path. Her power lies in her optimism and ability to spread good feelings to others. The bee will help you warm the hearts of others and make authentic relationships that will last any testing time.

Omil's spiders

Spider symbolises mystery, power and growth. She shows that thoughts become things and how to weave our lives wisely. She shows us how to use words to manifest positive change. Spider shows us how to become master manifestors by combining heart and mind to bring about our deepest wishes. She also lends determination and perseverance to anyone struggling to reach their goals.

Jimji's dragonfly

Dragonfly represents the subconscious mind and the inspiration we gain when day dreaming, musing or meditating. Dragonfly tells us to pay attention to our desires.

Dragonfly's power lies in her ability to alter states of consciousness at will. She knows life is an illusion created in the mind of the perceiver. She reminds us to live life to its fullest and always visualise positive outcomes.

Journey to meeting your clan totem

Sit or lie in a safe comfy place. Close your eyes. Focus on your breathing. Imagine yourself in a large, beautifully lit, cave. There are luxurious rugs and paintings adorning the walls, beautiful scents surround you. This is a safe, sacred place. You can hear the gentle running of water from further inside the cave. You walk towards the healing sound. You come to an open space. Above you, high up, is an opening in the cave which lets the sunlight in from the world above, surrounding you are tropical plants of all sizes, colours and scents, there is a large crystal clear pool before you. You sit by its edge. You can feel the water's vibrations beneath you; you are calm, warm and safe. In your mind ask for your clan totem to approach you. Beside you, a large flower opens to reveal the perfect animal totem who wants to impart some helpful knowledge to you. You are calm, warm, and safe. Take a moment to receive the message.

(It may come in words, music, colours, feelings, or a simple knowing.)

Thank the animal spirit. You watch it leave knowing you can call on it again if you need its help, knowledge, or power. You stand up and walk back into the cave. Once inside you hear music, faint and beautiful. You feel excited and decide to follow the music. You are led out of the cave and deep into a forest. You notice a stag and the music stops. You regard each other. There is the sound of a horn, which blows three times in the distance ~ a brilliant flash of inspiration hits you, an idea you can use once you return. The stag runs off into the forest, you lose sight of him and wish him well. You turn and notice a small door carved into a tree, you approach and touch the door which swings open, you enter and are immediately showered in a brilliant golden light. You awake, you are back inside your body. Wriggle those toes and stretch those fingers. Open your eyes and write down your findings straight away!

Day Fifteen

Who the Hell are You?

Your task for today is simply to read and complete the activities in this chapter. Sounds simple eh? Yeah. But, it may take time and courage. You need to remember to keep an open mind and keep breathing. You are about to reveal yourself.

Few of us know who we are in our totality. But you, after all these magical activities, should be in a more powerful position of knowing. You will be feeling a larger part of yourself unfurling, it is a beautiful special time for you. You are starting to bloom. The question is who are you after this awakening, how do you deepen its profoundness and create lasting change?

Today we are now going to look at who you think you are. I say think, because how we view ourselves is highly subjective and often different to what the outside world thinks of us. If you asked ten people to line up and asked them who is Alex Clarke, my former-husband is going to answer differently to my co-workers and both differently from me. So whose opinion matters? You got it, you're own. Only by owning your perception of yourself can you create a meaningful existence that satisfies you. I know, I know you're thinking of a million buts and a million exceptions. Your tummy is filled with butterflies and wasps; you're feeling that to be fully you will require loss, pain, and judgement. Go at your own pace. You are safe. There is no aspect of you that cannot be expressed safely.

Shadows, ideals and somewhere in the middle is the authentic

The ideal self

So there is you. Safe you, average you, twin suit and nice work's hairdo you. She wears flats instead of heels, worries about calories, organic hummus and the latest spray tanning methods. She is not out of place anywhere because she tries hard to be acceptable, to make connections, to be a member of her peer group. She is watchful of trends, observes moods and opinions, she is a good person but she is afraid. She lives with a creeping sensation that she is going to be found out. She is a chameleonesque fraud. She is the ideal self.

The ideal self is the idol version of who we are, or should be. I'm shuddering as I write *should*. It is the singular most toxic word in the psychological dictionary. Yuck. yuck yuck! Anyway the ideal self is herself an archetype. She is all the personality traits we like about ourselves, want for ourselves and value in others – she is kind or crazy depending on what you value. Even her likes and dislikes are idealised, she likes baking or perhaps knitting, kite-flying or train spotting (whatever you believe turns you on). The ideal self is different for each of us and is formed by our social circle and social upbringing.

The authentic real self

The authentic self is simplicity. She is you in the moment. She is your present self and can be recognised in the feeling of harmony, peace and love. She is everything you are and all your possibility. She strives for expansion through joy and love and is constantly looking, feeling and moving in that direction. The ideal self can get in her way ... as can the shadow self.

The shadow self

She sounds a bit scary doesn't she? But in reality the shadow self is merely all the bits of personality and behaviour we dislike, disapprove of, judge, or have ever been punished for. She is the inner demon – the lazy, cake gorging, sex-crazed hedonist. (Well, mine is anyway) and is often the opposite of your ideal self.

Inner conflict

You can now see how it works can't you? These three selves are in constant dialogue, they barter, cajole, bully, manipulate and shout, and all with the same goal in mind: to protect you; to keep you safe from the outside world and its inhabitants (who are also playing the same game with themselves too). Let's not be too hard on ourselves, we are social creatures and there is a lot of illusion out there. We are told fitting in is the same as being loved and that being loved is the same as feeling safe. This is an illusion. People connect with what is authentic within a person ~ even if we are covering up that side. We connect energetically, and no matter how hard we try we can hide our vibrations. Our social norms, constructs and expectations do not necessarily enable or encourage authenticity, human expansion or growth. So there the battle begins. It never ends. Every decision big or small goes to the counsel of the selves for discussion. The trick is to reach consensus and we do that through creatively mediating the meeting (see creative mediation below). This all sounds a bit serious and a little unusual doesn't it? I guess it is. Bear with the ideas. Stick at the unravelling and the wings you unveil will sparkle like glittery starlight under a full moon.

Exploring who you are

Firstly draw the outline of a person. Then list ten things you aspire to be or want to achieve in your life. I then want you to go back to look at your prayer to yourself. Examine your words. Cut them out. Decorate them. And then, stick them where you think they belong on the body.

How does it look? Don't worry if it's a bit messy, you are probably still believing that you are not creative, but that thought will be rapidly diminishing. This shape is your ideal self. Say hello. Maybe you want to give her a name? She is one of the barriers to you feeling better, look at her. Read the words you have chosen. Feel them. Let the words resonate so deep within you. How do you feel? Do you understand?

You see, even with our best intentions, we can place expectations on ourselves which we think will help us feel better, achieve our goals, or be more lovable. The ideal self can be a huge provocateur of shame, disappointment and even self-loathing.

Fae friend experience

I'd been working in health and social care for thirty years. I'd been everything from a social worker to a youth worker. I deeply valued myself for being empathic, helpful and loving. But over the years I started to feel myself becoming angry and angrier, I encounter difficult people (whether colleagues or service users) and would feel like throttling them. I used to go home and hate myself; I would wonder why on earth I felt so uncaring. It was horrible; I started to drink, not much, just a glass of wine a night trying to shove away my feelings of failure. Then I started creative mediating and working with my different selves, it helped. I started to care for myself and it helped me care for others.

~ Ali, 49

Once we have judged ourselves and our behaviour by the ideal self's measuring stick we feel lousy and because we feel lousy we are more likely to behave in ways we disapprove of and so the circle is completed and we experience stuckness.

Okay okay, sounds a bit bleak I know. But it's about to get brighter. Look back at your collage of words. Explore their meaning, drill down into their heart. Some words like 'loving', 'nice' and 'kind' can be devils in disguise. What do you actually mean by them? What have they motivated you to do? What was the outcome? Are they helping you feel better? Are they helping you achieve what you want? If the answer is yes, keep them. If the answer is no, then it is time to find new language.

In contrast the shadow self is all the parts of yourself that you have hidden or crushed to be accepted into mainstream society. Everything from wanting to scratch your bum in public to punch traffic wardens gets pushed into the shadow-making cauldron. What is cooked up is just as much, if not more, of a barrier to your wellbeing than the ideal self. Why? Because the ideal self has one thing going for it, you are aware of its demands. The shadow self is unconscious. It manoeuvres and manipulates us in sneaky cat-like ways. The shadow is slinky and slippery; 9 times out of 10 you won't even hear her whisper directions in your ear.

Unlike the ideal self, the shadow is also home to other aspects of yourself that float on an unconscious level. In particular your creativity; your faerie essence; your passion, drive and magical ability. You need this shadow to emerge into the light of your authentic self. When you bridge the gap, your faerie essence will emerge. Your creative self will awaken, motivate and empower you. You will move in the direction of your heart's desire with speed and precision. Of course we don't want all aspects of the shadow; some things are put in the bottom drawer for a reason. I'm in no way saying that your most negative aspects (whatever they may be) are always safe to unleash onto the world or indeed yourself. However, that is why I wrote this book, to help you sort the wheat from the chaff.

I want you to repeat the exercise you used to explore the ideal self with your shadow self. Write down all the things you fear you might be, the things you work hard to hide, the things you feel bad about or judge in others. Cut out these words and put them together in the shape of a person, please, give her a name. Look at her. Listen to the words in your mind. How do you feel? Remember you are safe, you are not alone. There are women all over the world reading this book, we are walking this path of awakening together. Eventually, future women and girls won't have to brave this path at all ~ we will be free to be whole. Be proud of you, you are a pioneer. You are healing your feminine ancestral line on all levels of time and space. Well done.

Creative mediation

How I conduct creative mediation in private sessions is different to how I will show you here, yet the principle is still the same. Your three selves (ideal, shadow and authentic) take centre stage to discuss your situation. In sessions we literally set a stage and I talk clients through the process, however you can do this at home as visualising the process is equally powerful. You are about to write a stage play for the selves. Don't worry, I will direct you. All you need to do is fill in the blanks.

Setting: the inner counsel meeting room. This can look elaborate or plain, it's up to you. The three selves are seated or standing. Note what they are wearing and their body language. The authentic self always steps forward first.

> Authentic self: The thing I want most in the world is …
> Ideal self: You can't possibly because …
> Shadow self: You could if you …
> Ideal self: You can't do that because …

Continue the dialogue until you reach a compromise suitable for all selves. If this is difficult you can introduce a new player ~ your faerie clan queen. What does she advise?

You can use this activity for any problem created by inner conflict. Simply take it to the inner counsel room for discussion. You will be in wonder at what you uncover about yourself and how easy it can be to solve even complex problems by using your creativity.

Day Sixteen

Totem Dance

Wow~wee! Yesterday saw a lot of inner work! I bet you had some pretty strange dreams last night, I hope you wrote them all down in your journal or are sharing them online at the Faerie Ring? Remember we are all each other's teachers and healers, sharing your experiences will help others understand their own.

Today we are raising our vibration using our Clan Totem's energy. Today you are going to dance with your totem energy leading the way. Smile! It's time to boogie~woogie!

1. Find a spot in the room where you can see your shadow on the wall.
2. Do three star jumps.
3. Stretch your arms out and call on your totem e.g. Oi butterfly! Be with Me! Power me up with your mojo please!
4. Do three more star jumps! Spin round ... let the feeling capture you!
5. Shout at the top of your lungs "I AM the GREATEST butterfly ever!" (or whichever totem is yours).
6. Do even more star jumps!
7. Continue until you wet yourself laughing.

Give yourself permission to have fun today. If you like to paint, write, sing or dance now is the time. Enjoy yourself. If you'd like to experiment with painting or music, try it out today. Don't worry about the result, just feel your way across the page with words or colour, sing out in song or sound. Feel better. If you have not yet found your creative outlet, pamper yourself with a bubble bath, nap, favourite movie, or big fat mug of tea. You deserve it you wonderful, brave, gorgeous creature! Sending you a hug of caramel scented love!

Day Seventeen

Journey to the Shadow Self

The aim of today is to make friends with your shadow self. As you now realise, you cannot become whole while denying your shadow love and affection. Your deeper nature is your essence; most of us have ignored, judged, shouted at and punished this inner nature for many years. You no longer need to fear your shadow. Remember, fear is the opposite of love and how do you behave when you are not loved? Think about it.

Your shadow once discovered normally takes the shape of a child. That's because the shadow forms when we are young when all our natural urges are pushed away and forgotten. The shadow is a neglected, afraid and abandoned child ~ sometimes she is pure fury.

Think about when you feel unloved, abandoned, judged, or forgotten. How do you wish others would treat you when you feel these things? Can you offer them to your shadow self? Can you be open to the possibility or loving her back to the light?

Meeting your shadow self

Close your eyes. Steady your breathing. You are safe and comfortable. Call on your faerie clan queen and totem to accompany you on your journey. Remember you are protected at all times. Allow yourself to relax. You can release all your anxieties. Breathe deeply. Let go of any tightness you may be feeling, surrender to the soft feeling in your muscles. You feel tranquil. Breathe out any nervousness and breathe in strength. Start to count backwards from 10. Allow your emotions to settle. Deep breathe. Release all thoughts, all ideas, all expectations. You are safe and warm. Just relax and enjoy the feeling of calm.

You can see yourself by a tall mountain. Led by your clan totem and followed by your faerie queen, you walk towards the mountain. Along the path are beautiful plants, tall grasses and friendly trees. You feel moss beneath your feet and the cool air against your skin. You come to a river. On the bank you notice an otter. You see how the otter is playing in the river's currents. You smile. The otter leaves the water and disappears down a hole in the river bank. Your Clan totem follows. Followed by your faerie clan queen you decide to follow. You peer into the hole and see a beautiful staircase leading downwards into the earth. You follow it, counting the steps down, backwards from 30, 29, 28, 27 ... until you reach 0. You come upon a candle lit room, there is small soft sofa with a large warm blanket draped across it; you climb onto the sofa and wrap yourself with the blanket.

Images pass before your eyes as if in a dream state. You watch with little emotion as you let the images come and go. You feel like a twig floating on a river, these thoughts, ideas and images pass by without harm; a youngster appears in your mind. She approaches you and asks you a question. You may or may not have the answer. The child doesn't mind either way and moves towards you. She wants to hug you. You feel an abundance of love for the child. You decide to embrace her and feel overwhelmed by peace, love and forgiveness. The child slowly disintegrates into you, you become one with her. You can feel your body heavy on the sofa. You listen to any feelings that rise up. You remain quiet and still, reflecting on how warm and safe you feel.

You hear a soft sound from on the staircase. You stand and approach the stairs to find glowing lights sitting on each step. You are delighted to see, flickering inside these lights, faerie wings. You can hear soft giggling. As you climb each step, this light, this pure faerie energy, is absorbed by your body and fills your entire being. You feel more and more happy, collecting light and joy as you climb the steps. You feel light, you can barely wait to arrive at the top and awaken fully back into your reality, whole, happy and refreshed! You count up from 1 to 30, until you reach the river. You climb out of the earth, new, reborn, happy and excited by your new revelations!

Take a bit of time to assimilate what has happened. Write it down; draw any symbols or pictures that came to you. Be good to yourself, be still and kind. You may feel moved to create a poem or song, do so. You may feel like a good cry, do so. Crying is a great way to release any negative energy, cleansing you and revitalising you for the next stage. You have done so well.

Try not to over analyse your experience. Let your intuitive right-brain take charge. There will be time for integration later, for now try to be in your feelings – they will be telling you much more than your intellect right now. Enjoy your insights. You are becoming all you were destined to be!

Day Eighteen

Code of Ethics

It's time to take a breather and put together all you have learned and discovered so far. We have been through a lot together haven't we? Go and get your faerie journal and review your progress. Have you managed to ritualise your changes ~ making them part of your everyday life? What have you found most enjoyable? Can you adapt the activities to better suit your personality? What has surprised you? Where have you seen the biggest positive changes?

Stay in this place of self-appreciation.

From this place of positive pride I want to introduce the concept of boundaries. Boundaries is a term often used in helping relationships or marriage counselling as a way of looking at safe, respectful, and yes helpful ways of maintaining separateness.

Establishing boundaries can also be a helpful way that the ideal self can communicate gently with our authentic and shadow self. Personal boundaries are our very own code of ethics; a guide to help us remember who we are and where we are going. The code should be achievable and personal ~ it should reflect you and have relevance to your journey. The code is also subject to change and adaptation once you discover new things about your world and your place in it.

How to create your code of ethics

Gather together some pictures, textiles, photos, paint and paper. Ask yourself the following questions and answer as truthfully as you can from your heart. Your code is designed to take the blurred edges of your personality and sharpen them, this way you will be reminded of the bigger picture of your journey's purpose. Answering the following questions will help you nail

68

down what you think is ethical and important in your life.

Which quote, song, or poem most represents how you view life?

What fills your heart with the most love? Family? Work? Travel? Etc …

What activities do you really need to avoid? (if you have heart disease, perhaps it is fatty foods).

If you could leave one sentence here for future generations, what would it be?

What or who inspires you?

Once you have answered these questions move on to creating your code, like my own personal one below. Play around with your ideas until they feel true and achievable. Then write the code on a card that you can place in your wallet to inspire you throughout the day.

My personal code

Today, I'll treat others how I wish to be treated.

I will use my words to bring smiles and laughter.

I will aim to write words that move me and others towards greater joy.

I will spend time with those I love and avoid those that do not have my best intentions at heart.

I use the word today as it gives us the opportunity to try again tomorrow. If, after a week, your code is not working i.e. making you feel empowered and successful, then change it. Do not hold on to ideas that you think *should* be working, simply replace them with things that will work. Experimentation is key. You are discovering what is right for you; the gauge will be what *feels* good.

Day Nineteen

Personal Heart Talisman

Now you have your code of ethics you are in a powerful position to start your next activity – re-scripting yourself. Before we move on to this, I'd like you to try the following fun exercise. Take a walk outdoors. Yep, put on your wellies if it's raining, take the kids if you fancy and while you are out keep your eyes open for a small stone. Once you stumble (hopefully, not literally) across one, bring it home. You should have some paint about the place, if not improvise with what you do have. Sit in your sacred place while stirring up your paint, think about all the people, places, artworks and animals that fill your heart will an abundance of love and joy. Now dip just your fingertip/nails into your paint and flick the colour onto your stone. Leave it to dry. Don't change the shape, don't try to perfect it, just accept it for what it is. This is your talisman; your heart talisman; representing your heart ~ unique and strong. You can carry it, leave under your pillow or place it in your sacred place. Whenever you feel wounded, scared or weak, simply return to your talisman and remember who you are.

Fae friend experience

I'm a rape survivor and this really helped. I placed my heart in a piece of silk and kept it in a small box under my bed. Whenever I had nightmares or flash backs I would get my heart out. It reminded me I still have it, no matter what.

~ Anon

Day Twenty

Re-scripting Yourself

The words we use to describe ourselves are vital to our wellbeing. As the immortal saying goes, thoughts become things and what we believe about ourselves becomes our reality. No matter how many times people try to convince us otherwise, our own mental processes will determine how we feel about ourselves. It's what's inside that counts in more ways than one. The words you use to define yourself will mirror how you feel about yourself. Choose your words wisely.

We have all chosen badly. We have all had rubbish days when beating up on ourselves seems the only logical conclusion to a series of bad choices and silly random acts of ice-cream eating (my bad) yet it can create a self-defeating cycle of profanity that reinforces and enables further poor decision making. And we don't want this! How will you ever feel worthy of good things heading your way if you constantly feel bad about yourself?

Evidence supports the idea that the words we use to describe ourselves carry weight. We often live to prove ourselves right, therefore the first step to changing how we feel about ourselves is to change how we speak about ourselves. Look back at your ideal and shadow-self activities. All these conflicting characteristics are how you view yourself. You now have the opportunity to re-write your self-image and start speaking about yourself and to yourself kindly, and with love.

Yes, this may require a bit of effort. I mean, how can you change how you speak about yourself if you have never really paid attention to your own self-talk?

Self-talk is automatic and subtle. For the next few days, slow down your inner conversations, pay attention to the internal dialogue. You may be surprised by what you hear.

Fae friend experience

I was stunned. I called myself stupid, not just once, but all the time! It was like my default setting when things went wrong
~ Sara, 28 (marketing assistant)

Very often self-talk will be a single word, sound, or phrase that is heavy with symbolism and elicits a strong emotional response. So for example looking in the mirror and saying 'eww' looking at your bank statement and saying 'oh god', tripping over the cat and saying 'stupid cow' (to yourself not the cat) these tiny statements may take some dissecting to discover what emotion they link with.

Self-talk can be helpful or unhelpful. Unhelpful self-talk will always perpetuate procrastination, avoidance and maintaining the status quo. Unhelpful self-talk will always leave you feeling worse and often defeated or hopeless.

Types of unhelpful self-talkers

Worriers

Worriers use the language of fear to inflate anxiety and keep the user in their comfort zone. Yes I know it feels real and justified, but so do the feelings elicited from horror movies. If you use the language of fear you are likely to anticipate the worst, overestimate the chances of humiliating yourself, disappoint others and experience tragedy happening to you and those you love. The most common phrases used by worriers are 'what if .... ' And 'oh no ... '

Bullies

Bullies use the language of evaluation and comparison. They constantly judge themselves by what others do, have or say. This type of self-talk is aimed at humiliating the user into better behaviours. It manifests in pointing out flaws, mistakes and failure in all-encompassing statements like 'you never get it right' and 'they can cope why can't you?' or/and 'you're so fat, stupid, ugly ... (insert your own insult here)'.

Saints

Saints disguise their bullying in motivational speeches that often promote unattainable god-like goals. They use the language of perfection to tell themselves their best efforts are not enough. Saints are often ambitious driven people ~ they also often burn out. Saints' favourite phrases include 'I should be able to ... ' and 'I must .... ' Or 'I have to .... '

Victims

Victims speak the language of defeat and hopelessness. This voice tells you how beyond help you are, that you are too damaged/broken/hurt to live a fulfilling life. The automatic language of victims normally starts with 'I'll never .... ' and 'what's the point' or 'that's okay for them but for someone like me ... '

Overcoming unhelpful self-talk

We all fall into one or more of these categories from time to time, it's only when you find yourself stuck there that you have a real challenge on your hands. Therefore, it's best to become aware of and tackle your inner-self-talk before you end up caged by it.

The best way to overcome such self-defeating statements is to use supportive statements instead. Yes, this sounds easier said than done. This is just because you are attached to your negative beliefs and believe them! You have been practicing believing them for years! Chances are the people and events in your life will be reinforcing these beliefs too. However, all your beliefs right now are just a result of habitual thinking. Today you can choose to practice another way. Here's how. When you are indulging in unhelpful self-talk, for example 'I'm so stupid' ask yourself the following questions:

Is this always true?
Am I being fair?
Will this thinking help me move forward?
Would I say this to someone I love dearly?

Writing magic words

After answering these questions you need to use magic words to re-empower ~ words designed to move you forward. Writing these statements is very personal. Here are some helpful tips to guide you into making them really positive and energetic!

Reversals: simply completely swapping the negative with its positive opposite. So avoid saying 'I am not stupid' (this holds the negative and your mind will always attach to the vibration of that word.) Instead say 'I am smart' and your energy will respond accordingly.

Make your magic statements in the present tense such as 'I let this feeling pass' rather than 'I'll be alright tomorrow'.

Own your statements with 'I' such as 'I am calm' rather than 'It will calm down.'

Try the stop technique. Shout stop! And stamp your foot at the same time. Then sing a nursery rhyme of your choice.

Become aware today of your negative self-talk. Tonight, bring to mind your most common terms and write some magic words to take into tomorrow. If you want to increase their power, repeat them throughout the day and combine them with deep feelings of joy, or peace, or happiness by following the short exercise below.

Powering up your magic words

Close your eyes and focus on your breathing. Take three deep breaths and call on your faerie queen and clan totem. They will be with you, keeping you safe at all times. Keep breathing calmly and gently. Now recall a time when you felt really good about yourself. (If you don't have one, imagine what it would feel like.) When you have that memory and are experiencing that feeling repeat your magic counterstatement to yourself while pressing your right ear lobe between your thumb and fingers. Now tomorrow when you need to use your magic words remember to press your ear lobe and your mind will remember all those happy, peaceful feelings from the night before and give you a taste of them in the present! Brilliant eh? You bet ya!

Day Twenty-one

Kneading your Needs

This book contains many permission slips and perhaps this one is the most important. I want you to think about what you are entitled to in life. What you are eligible for simply because you were born. This is a large question. Contemplate it. What are you entitled to without having to be or do anything in return? What should you receive despite all you judge in yourself? Duna clan are good at this task, they know their rights and often fight to uphold these rights for others too. Having difficulty? Ask a Duna fae. Failing that, check out the list of human needs and place them in order of importance.

A selection of human needs

- to express emotion
- to rest
- to be nurtured
- to be loved unconditionally
- to be safe ~ both physically and emotionally
- to have shelter
- to have freedom ~ to be different and self-directing
- to be financially secure
- to have meaningful friendships
- to be given attention
- to be respected
- to receive validation
- to be able to self-express
- to give and receive intimacy
- to be able to demonstrate sexual expression
- to have fun and play

- to make a meaningful contribution to community and/or society
- to belong
- to be heard
- to achieve a sense of accomplishment and/or progress
- to experience creativity
- to trust

Look at your list. What did you leave off? What did you scoff at and disagree with? I am going to propose that the needs you ignored are the needs you are neglecting right now. I also bet my bottom dollar they are the things you were chastised for as a child, or by your first love, your first friend, boss, teacher or mentor. At some point you have been told these things are not important. Do you remember when?

Fae friend experience

It was totally unexpected, it just appeared, I was so angry. Boom! I felt silly at the thought of needing attention. Attention! Me. It's the one thing I can't stand in others, I hate it, that 'look at me look at me' I felt silly and then rage at the silliness. It took me a while to realise the anger was at my mum all those years ago telling me off for 'attention seeking' I felt sad, all I really wanted was her to be proud of me.
~ Kate, 25 (musician)

Your inner faerie has no fear acknowledging her needs. And her acknowledgement dances with wisdom. The wisdom to know that although she has these needs they may not always be met ~ this dance buffers her from the disappointment and despair of living in the human world of polarity.

You will have certain needs that are not always met. Knowing your needs means you can prepare for the difficulties encountered when you feel let down. You see you have choices too. You can beat yourself up for having the need. You can tell yourself the need was not a valid need in the first place. Or more helpfully, you can try to fulfil the need yourself. It's also a good idea to learn how to nurture yourself in the disappointment, rejection, anger and sadness that comes from having a need neglected. There is a chapter on managing difficult emotions that may help you with those feelings; the ritual on forgiveness will be helpful too.

For now, it is time to get yourself a bill of rights! Claiming your entitlements is empowering and declares you are worth something ~ it's like shouting to the universe 'I love me!'

Bill of rights exercise

Take three of the needs you would enjoy offering to yourself. Write them down on a small piece of card and place this in your bag or purse. You can also write a larger one too and place it where you can see it daily. Read it out loud. Believe it. Become it. Be it! The example below is to help you get started, when you finish share it with your faerie friends on the Facebook faerie ring group.

My Bill of Rights
I have a right to express my emotions.
I have a right to express my opinion.
I have a right to express my sexuality.
I have a right to change my mind.

Day Twenty-two

Re-scripting the World

Did you buy a newspaper today? Perhaps you watched the news? It pays to be informed right? Think for a moment about how you view the world. Ask yourself these questions and answer as truthfully as possible ~ don't double-think your answers, use your first instinctual response.

- Is the world fair?
- Is there enough to go around? (Love? Food? Money?)
- Is life easy?
- Are people around you always doing their best?
- Is the world safe?

Yes, by now you know I am going to ask you to reframe the statements so you can use them to re-script your opinion of the world. This will allow greater opportunity for joy, stress-relief and creative flow. If you are living in a heightened state of stress and fear brought on by media it really is not good for your health, wealth or happiness. Opt to make-believe the world is kind. It will change your life.

Finding it difficult? You are not alone. I had to get rid of my television! Ask yourself how being informed is affecting your wellbeing. Then ask yourself is being informed helping the current world situation? If you worry about world hunger, animal rights, crime victims, set up a monthly direct debit to a reputable charity, run a marathon, or volunteer overseas or in your local soup kitchen. In the time it takes to become informed, you could have chosen a charity or cause and given then an hour of your time. Imagine how quickly the world's situation would change if we all did that?

This can be especially hard if, like me, you have experienced someone else's actions ripping holes in your own personal choices. I'm a rape survivor. But becoming informed about rape statistics and reading newspapers didn't help me survive. Reaching out to other women survivors did. There is great power in deciding how you view your world. Not your perpetrator, not your parents, not the media or political party.

Again, here are the magic questions to help you challenge your beliefs. Remember you are safe to change and now is the time. The universe is your friend and your faerie clan are always there to support your process. Ask yourself:

1. Is this belief always true?
2. Is this belief helpful to you?
3. Are you willing to chance being wrong about your present belief?

The last question is pivotal. If the answer is yes, I want you to write down what you think is true of the world and then create counterstatements using the method you used in chapter 20 to re-script yourself. If the answer is no, that is ok. You don't feel ready and the important aspect of this book is to give you the power to say a loud guilt-free no. And whether you have said yes or no to this exercise, be proud of you. I am.

Day Twenty-three

Conflict Resolution the Faerie Way

Today we talk other people. Come on, be honest, you have met resistance haven't you? There must have been a few moments of conflict over the past few days. Those around you might be finding your new venture troubling in the least and some may even find it infuriating. You may have been accused of some things like err, let's say, selfishness? Craziness? Not living in the real world. Pah! The real world is full of average ~ you are not average. The real world is filled with critics ~ the people who live empty lives punctuated by commenting on other people who are living. You are not a commentator; you have been laying foundations to become an adventurer, a liver of life and a lover of experience. You are becoming extraordinary and you deserve credit!

Conflict resolution the faerie way is very simple. Don't fight. Don't disagree. Don't sweat it. Keep on keeping on. People have a right to be different and we never convince them with words that we are right, we only ever convince them with our energy. Your energy will feel different, they will either want you to revert (and will try every trick in the book to get you to switch) or want to know your secret. Keep the seekers of the secret. Ignore the reverters. This will be hard if they are very close and you love them, so here are a few tips straight from the Omil clan who are wise enough to see patterns in others and show us how not to wear their issues as our own.

- Don't preach your new way of life, just live it.
- Keep the philosophy of you are ok, I'm ok in mind at all times.

- Know you cannot control other people's reactions to your truth.
- Be empathic, seeing people we love changing can be scary, reassure them that you still love them.
- Assert that you cannot live an unhappy life to make others feel safe, loved or needed.
- Remember they are just trying to be right and you have learnt the futility of this activity, right?

If the conflict is starting to really upset you and interfere with your process try the following activity.

Faery peace-keeping

Close your eyes and start the 4 by 4 breathing. Visualise the person you are having conflict with sitting in front of you. They have a golden light in their chest. You notice a similar light in your own. The lights grow bigger until they leave your bodies. You see the lights meet in the space before you. Watching in awe and wonder you notice inside the light are two faeries. Each faerie is holding the other by the hands. You watch them embrace and fly back to their respective homes; one to your home, the other to your friend's. You recognise you are both doing your best. You can feel relieved in the knowledge that the relationship will take the highest path towards a helpful conclusion.

Day Twenty-four

Teddies, Toys and Fun!

Think back to when you were a child. For some of you this may be difficult, childhood is not always the best of times, but I only want you to look at one aspect ~ your favourite toys. Mine were Jem dolls and an elephant called, well, Ellie. Those dolls brought about my love of storytelling and in particular theatre. Storytelling on stage is transient and no two shows are the same ~ a bit like our own experiences of living similar events.

> She'd sit for hours making up improvised 'shows' with the dolls. They were no longer Jem characters they were her creation. Stories went on for days, they were our escape.
> ~ Tess Clarke, my Twin Sister

Ellie was my protector; a hersh (what I called something neither male nor female when I was a child). It was one of my best companions and now sits on a shelf in my mind having been physically lost over the years. With Ellie beside me I was invincible. A feeling much needed growing up in a haunted house that often went bump in the night. Look back. What did you gain from the toys you played with? Now with your adult eyes you will be able to see what they taught you about the value of play.

Now remember how your favourite toys made you feel. What is that feeling? A sense of freedom? Love? Companionship? When was the last time you felt like that? It is time to rekindle that childhood magic by taking a shopping spree. Go and find that childhood toy on eBay (the king of retro toys) rummage in second hand shops or put a shout out on freecycle. Once you find a similar toy or if you are really lucky the same model ~ close the curtains, sit on the floor and play.

Animal toys

Favourite stuffed animals are a great indicator of our animal spirit guide. In certain shamanic traditions animal spirit guides accompany us to this realm as they resonate so closely with our own personalities. We often have two or more (some believe as many as two per chakra!). One represents our higher self, one our lower (sometimes referred to as the shadow). These are not better or worse ~ they are just valued by us differently.

The higher animal spirit guide is often an animal we feel a natural affinity with. The lower (shadow) may elicit a phobic response as its own traits and behaviours we do not want to associate with.

Fae friend experience

I had a deep fear of sharks. In particular their cold, dead eyes. Me and Alex talked about the shark, its habits, its evolution. I began to shake and feel sick; I remember saying they just seemed so unfeeling and inhuman and she asked 'why do you think they need to be like that?' And at once I said 'to survive' and then I came to the understanding that when I felt under threat I became detached like the shark, to survive. And that has been a blessing.

~ Julie, 36

Animal mask activity!

Many of us celebrate Halloween with a masquerade of masks. This dates back thousands of years to the ancient Celtic festival of Samhain. This was the time to celebrate our ancestor's lives, their journey to the otherside and the guidance they still offer us through our intuition, dreams and day-time musings. During Samhain, Celtic shamans wore costumes consisting of their clan animal skins ~ often performing ceremonies to contact their ancestors to predict the coming year's fortunes. Now if literally playing with childhood toys is too much to ask of you (but seriously, you really are never too old to be silly) mask-making may be a more accessible activity. Doing this with friends is a hoot, especially if you make your costumes for your faerie birthday party as it adds another dimension to the celebration!

What you need:

Crepe paper (in the colour of your animal).

Card board (any, even an old cereal box will do).

PVA glue (as it dries transparent).

A gorgeous ribbon (in your favourite colour).

Glitter, paint and feathers ~ colours depending on what animal you are making.

(All the above are available from craft stores and most super-markets.)

1. Draw a circle on the card that will be large enough to cover your face. (Or just big enough to cover your eyes if making a bird mask.)
2. Make two holes for the eyes and two holes for the ribbon so you can secure the mask to your head when finished (Or you can attach a stick to hold your mask in front of your face if tying it would feel too claustrophobic.)
3. Cut out any added shapes (such as horns, beaks, ears etc) from the cardboard.
4. Attach your add-ons to the circle with PVA glue.
5. Take strips of your crepe paper and glue them onto your mask, keep layering the paper on top of each other until a nice texture and colour is achieved.
6. Leave to dry for a couple of hours before returning to paint it. Only get your brushes out if you feel the mask needs a splodge or two. If it doesn't, decorate with glitter and

feathers to suit. Attach the ribbon or stick and leave to dry overnight before wearing!

Day Twenty-five

Colourful Emotion

Today is all about colour, emotion and self-expression the abstract way. You are going to get messy! The Frey will love this activity as it is all about colour and free-expression. This is free art, fast art, art without engaging the conscious mind. This helps us to express our feelings in our artwork without censorship. Don't plan a picture. The idea is just to choose colours. This is not as unusual as it seems, the emotional language of colour has even entered our vocabulary such as 'seeing red' for rage or being 'green with envy'. We often speak of bright cheerful colours as well as sad or dull ones. We even have 'grey' days that result in feeling 'the blues'.

Fae friend experience
To me yellow creates an energetic image that radiates feelings of hope and joy. I need bold colours in my art. Primary colours fill me with energy and when I use them I am automatically uplifted.
~ Mia, 27 (faerie artist)

We live in a world of pastels and grey. Nature is not beige. Nature is hootching with explosive rich textured colour; she is brazen, uninhibited and shameless. Your activity today is all about expressing nature's wildness. You will do it by following your feeling onto the canvas, paper, wall or backyard ~ wherever you want to create your emotional masterpiece!

Firstly find a quiet space and focus on your breathing. Now draw your attention to how you feel, where is this feeling? What colour is it? What shape? What speed?

Take your paint and transfer this feeling onto paper. When the feeling within you changes, stop painting. Literally stop. Don't tamper or change your creation. The picture is perfect and complete. What feeling has slid into place within you now? Repeat the exercise as many times as you want.

Keep a record in your faerie journal of all the interesting thoughts, visions, colours and creations that flood you today. We would love to see your paintings at the Faerie Ring Facebook group too!

Day Twenty-six

Photo Stories

Whether enduring the school run, rushing to work, job-centre or jogging with the dog, morning is the best time for today's project. Today you will find beauty in the mundane. The aesthetic in your everyday life ~ it is everywhere. Just follow your usual routine but look for at least ten photo opportunities, yes, ten. There are more, but ten will do this morning. Take the photos and then forget about them until this evening.

Once the evening arrives, upload your photographs, or flick through them. What have you discovered? What is the emotion you are feeling looking at your beautiful morning? Log your discoveries down in your journal. Do you understand the importance of this activity? Will you repeat it? Share your results with us.

Fae friend experience

Looking for things made me aware; it brought me right into the present. Beauty became really important and once I wanted to see it, it was as if the universe said 'get a load of this!' I now do this every Sunday, out of all the exercises this one alone changed my life, it has shown me in a very physical way how what we focus on becomes what we see.

~ Laura, 31 (school teacher)

Day Twenty-seven

Inner and Outer Sound

I was a silent child. Some say an observer, but often it was fear of what would occur if I vocalised my experience that kept me quiet. Through my adult life I have been tripped easily back into silence and more than anything else this has been my greatest challenge. Many people have stepped on my path to teach me how to use my voice; some of that teaching was harsh. My voice has remained hidden and protected like the seeds of a flower inside a bud. I am journeying with my voice to freedom.

All things are vibrations, from cells to bones, bones to tone. Your voice resonates with the sound of your soul. Your inner voice is part of how you communicate your vibrations with the world. Sound changes matter and matter changes sound.

I say part because a lot of our sounds cannot be heard but they are still in existence. Our senses are not an adequate indicator of our world. A dog's greater sense of smell and hearing proves that our senses are not up to the massive job of translating reality. Dogs use those smells and sounds which are not perceived by humans, yet they must be there otherwise the dog wouldn't react.

Experiments have shown that the very molecular structure of water changes when music is played! Also when water is placed in glass bottles with words on the outside the molecular structure of the water changes. Words of love, gratitude and abundance create symmetry whereas words of hate, anger, and destruction create disordered patterns. This is interesting considering that our bodies are 90 per cent water isn't it?

It is your sounds that make you fully multi-dimensional as sound is not physical, but creates and affects reality. Sound vibration is a large part of anchoring you with your creative core

~ it's your furnace, your sun, your inner burning star. Your inner faerie will be awakened by your soul song. Make your words tempting to your inner self and you will unfurl the power and knowledge within you, which has the potential to melt and mould reality.

Before you go to bed tonight, write down what you most want to heal, achieve, or experience and tape it onto a glass/bottle of water. This is your very first magic potion. When you wake, you are going to say what is written on your taped message. You are going to drink your sacred water. Note down how it feels to know your vibration is changing in line with your desire.

Now, bring your message to mind. I want you to sing it in your head, then hum it out loud, now sing it, belt it right out!

Until your faerie birthday I want you to refrain from any music that makes you feel anything but uplifted and positive. This may be hard, especially if you are a musician. However, this is a once in a lifetime opportunity to experiment with changing your vibration from where it is right now to where you want it to be. You deserve to give yourself that chance; it is, after all, not long until you are reborn.

Day Twenty-eight

Awakening your Inner Faerie Ritual

Tomorrow you will be reborn with great big glittery wings and a shiny smile! You'll remember this birth time. It's going to be very special, for you are very special. You are magnificent, you are a bundle of expansive joy, and you are ready. Today you are going to construct a faerie den. It can be bold, simple, posh or poor. Mine was a blanket over two chairs. Others have gone to great lengths and hired yurts! Just make sure it is comfortable for you are going to sleep here tonight. Yes, tonight you are going to reach back over your experience and write down what you have discovered. You are going to recall when you smiled, laughed and were overcome with joy and self-love. You'll recall how you have hugged yourself in the dark times and when you have stood close to madness and bowed your head in honour. Tonight you will merge with your inner faerie. You will acquire the power of self and become your own great mother, your own faerie queen. Tonight you will remember and awaken. Tomorrow you will be a new whole creative self beyond all you have been before.

Awakening your Inner Faerie Ritual Journey

You need:

a pen
candle
incense
this book
Don't light the candle inside the den unless it is safe to.

Climb inside your den and get comfy, I hope you have lots of cushions and blankets; you want to feel warm and cosy. Light your candle. You can light some incense and play some gentle music too. Bring your breathing to a calm steady pace. Call on your faerie queen and clan totem. Feel them both close by, supporting and loving you. Remember, you are safe to let go, you are safe to leave all your worries and fears in the past. You are safe to become your whole self. Your inner light will attract nothing but joy, love and abundance to you. You and your loved ones are protected on levels of time and space.

You are about to chant your clan's sacred sound. This sound will create a vibrational shift in your environment to empower your transition. As you chant you may even see a large white sphere accompanying the sound, emanating from you outwards beyond your aura. So now begin your chant. Start the sound in your mind until you feel comfortable to verbalise it, mind chanting still evokes vibrational change. Do your best, enjoy the process and smile as you feel the vibrational change all around you.

Once you feel your shape is established you can stop chanting. Focus again on your breath. It is time to speak your intention to the universe, state:

I am the creator. Worlds exists within me, extend from me, through time and space, realm to realm, dimension to dimension. My inner Faerie is my outer Faerie, my inner creator is my outer creator, I am whole and complete, I am awake, I am ready, I am beginning, I am on the brink, I am close, I am emerging, I am pure divine ratio, pure vibration, pure creation, pure manifestation, pure love, I am, I am, I am.

Close your eyes. Let your heart rate settle and your breathing become peaceful and calm. You are comfortable. Start to count backward from 100, 99, 98, 97 … you see before you a wild place. It is filled with huge tall bluebells with giant thick stalks. The scent of flowers makes you feel slightly giddy and excited. You can hear beautiful song and laughter. Looking around through the forest of flowers you see your clan totem and those of the other clans. They are huge, but friendly. They wait to celebrate your emergence. You smile. Walking through the flowers you come upon a uniquely beautiful radiant flower. Carved into its stem is a symbol. You reach out and place your hand onto it, the green of the stem parts like two velvet curtains and inside, seated on a thrown of leaves and crafted twigs, is your faerie self. She is smiling. You are smiling too. You walk towards her and she reaches out and takes your hands. You stand eye to eye, still smiling. She embraces you and you are overwhelmed by love and peace as you feel her step inside you. Everything within you, every molecule, cell, synapse, organ, vessel, bone and memory greet your faerie self with gratitude and recognition. You can feel your muscles become stronger, your breath steadier, your vision sharper and hearing clearer. You are flooded with eager projects to start, people you want to meet and missions you want to complete. You remember all the truth of yourself and it feels magnificent. You see a staircase leading further and further up the flower and run towards it with excitement. You run faster and faster up the winding stair case until you find yourself stood on the petals surrounded by all the clan totems, you feel how proud they are of you and your heart is filled with appreciation for all that was you, all that is you and all you are about to become. Suddenly you feel a warm sensation burst across your shoulders and out unfurls the most glorious pair of glittering colourful faerie wings. You are overjoyed and spring off the petal into the sky as the clan totems bid you good luck. You open your eyes. You can see the candle flame before you. You are whole, complete and home.

Watch the flame, let your focus soften, close your eyes and continue to breathe, if any thoughts rise acknowledge them, tip your hat but then let them go, no judgement, no fear, no attachment. Let them all float free. Return to your breathing. This time with each out breath, rock forward and state the word *awake* repeatedly, using the breath, movement and the sound to lose connection with the material and enter the ethereal. Keep going for as long as you can. When you are tired, stop and state, 'I am awake. I am, so I am awake'. Open your eyes and look into the flame, then close your eyes. When you are ready, take your pen, write down what you have remembered or discovered while on this journey into the faerie kingdom that is you. Well done my fae friend. No matter where I am, I am sending you a warm cosmic hug. Sleep well x

Day Twenty-nine

Faerie Birthday Party Time!!

Good morning gorgeous soul! How did you dream? How do you feel? Do you feel with all that newness sparkling and spangling within your veins? Do you feel ready to get some decorations up, get some music on, put on your faerie regalia and throw your party? Of course you do! You have reached the finish line and you have given yourself the gift of a lifetime, the present of a whole you. A more rounded, more glittery, more magical creative self. You are in a powerful position right now. Now is where your future is built, one feeling at a time. You know how to move forward. You know what is right for you. You have all the power you need to structure your life in the way you know will bring you the greatest self-expression, personal power and peace of mind. You know the joy is within you. The love that powers each cell, atom and molecule of you is leading you to where you need to be next. Listen to what you need, recognise how much you have changed. Enjoy your party, you have earned it!

But that is not all. Oh no. To keep your effervescent faerie self-satisfied you have to keep her occupied. Why not try the Faerie challenge? The challenge of taking on a creative project and completing it over the next twelve months? Perhaps you have always wanted to sing? Act, play an instrument? Or like me, maybe you want to write a book? Now you can. What are you waiting for? Let us at the Faerie Ring know what you are brave enough to choose!

In the next chapter we will speak to some fae friends who, powered by their connection to faerie, have fluttered before you and will inspire some elemental mission. As for me, I wish you happiness, creativity, joy and abundance and just a pinch of mischief with every flit-flutter of your shiny new wings.

Day Thirty

Inspiring Fae Friends

'I create from a faerie I imagine, never sketch her, she looks better in my dreams.'
~ Kaerie Faerie (faerie doll-maker)

Dancing into the wild places can fill a girl with trepidation. You are not alone, here are some highly creative, wonderfully inspiring faerie filled women who know what you are going through and want to offer you their words of wisdom and encouragement ...

I've always believed in and loved faeries and anything otherworldly. When I was pregnant with my 3rd son Marley, I began to draw and paint faeries. My hormones were desperate to bring out the more feminine side of my nature, and I also expressed my creative side by designing and making otherworldly clothing.

I was given the opportunity to sing with my band Malachite at Karen Kay's 3 Wishes Faery Festival in Cornwall in 2010, which helped further to connect with my faery gifts, and to meet like-minded faery folk. As a result of this I have had huge encouragement from my faery friends to continue creating songs and faery clothes and crafts.

I see energy bubbles and definitely feel a presence when creating songs especially. I even have a photo taken by a faery friend at 3 Wishes Faery Festival in 2011 showing my 'Faery Guide' who I feel has been with me a long time, and is the one who helps me with song writing, as I have been told by a Faery psychic.

The advice I would give to future faery fans is ~ don't be afraid to express your authentic nature, go and experience Faery Festivals and Faery Balls and surround yourself with Faery folk of all kinds who will help you to express your inner fae!
~ Babz Hewlett-Beech (fashion designer and lead singer with Malachite)
Check out Babz's work by visiting:
www.etsy.com/shop/MOODSHIFTCLOTHING

* * *

My first experience with the faeries occurred after I'd attended a festival in the Midlands. I'd gotten home quite late and as I was going to bed, there was a gnome in my bedroom! I saw him next to my bed nearest my window and he was grumpy, in the most adorable fashion, and was busy grumbling to himself picking up my clothes off the floor. As I lay down on the bed still quite euphoric over the evening, I saw Pan playing his pan-pipes.

After this, Queen Mab, Queen of the Faeries made frequent visits to me and it was during these times where she requested that I become a Faerie Priestess and work in her honour to teach many people about the faeries. She assured me that after she had initiated me I would be shown the way at all times.

Working with the faeries hasn't suddenly taken away all my problems – on the contrary. I believe that I have faced more challenges, yet I have also been given the strength and tools to get through them and come out a much stronger person. Since working with the faeries I have been on an amazing journey where I became a columnist for FAE magazine. I've also seen my confidence grow. I was always very much a wall flower, but over the years I've watched myself bloom and grow and honestly feel like a fully fledged, confident and empowered Priestess now. I love the work that I do, which includes writing for various publications, recording podcasts for an international faerie and angel magazine and radio network. I have also started a life coaching business whereby I was guided by the faeries and my life experiences to help empower women in the twenty-first century using "celestial" energy.

Whenever I have a big decision to make, I consult the angels and the faeries. I like to get a perspective from the heavenly realm as well as a more grounded and brutally honest perspective from the faeries. The thing with the faeries is that I know they will always tell me how it is. Take for instance a relationship I was in during 2012. It wasn't a healthy relationship, but I was guided during meditation by the faeries to stay there a little longer and that my significant birthday would provide the answers for me. This was confirmed time and again when I consulted oracle cards. It was my twenty-fourth birthday that year and had always had a personal significance to me since I was a child. On my birthday I discovered that my partner was not who I thought he was, and in the proceeding few days I uncovered the emotional and mental, and also physical abuse he'd subjected me to. After a couple of months of healing with a lot of support, I found the strength and power within me to stand with my head held high. The faeries showed me how important that relationship was for me, they showed me that it was time that I stopped being a doormat in ALL areas of my life. Since then, I haven't allowed anyone to walk all over me, and I don't intend to start doing so ever again. This was how my "Celestial Life Coaching" came about. So, the faeries have shown me the pathway for career purposes, relationships, self-growth, self-worth, self-esteem and also how strong I can be. They do this with everyone they can help.

I absolutely feel faeries when I work creatively. I see them hovering over my shoulder and they get very excited. I also feel their presence when I get an idea, it's like having your personal PA with you at all times constantly feeding back to you their opinion. I've had some ideas and they've not discouraged me, but they have made me aware of an even better method for doing something, and also better opportunities coming my way. If I feel that they aren't around me and I need a little creative help, I simply call upon my Faerie Guardian (Like a guardian angel), and Queen Mab for help.

I would say to any future faerie fan, the best thing you can do is listen to your faerie heart. Before acting, think, 'If I were a faerie how would I feel about this happening?' I would also have to say that it is so important to stay grounded. I'm lucky that as well as my faerie work I have other avenues where I work and literally 'escape from faerieland', because as much as the faeries love us – and they do – they really want us to love and live our earthly lives with mindfulness for the faerie realm. This means at times being a human earthly being (however boring that may feel – it's vital to our spiritual growth), and getting on with the daily chores, although the faeries will help us if we ask. But be warned, they will do it their way, and their way will be a lot more fun and perhaps slightly chaotic – but at least you'll have a real good time.
~ Dawn *Aurora* Brierley, aka The Faerie Whisperer (columnist with FAE magazine)
Check out Dawn's work by logging on:
www.FaerieWhisperer.co.uk

* * *

Before encountering my first faery creature I did not believe in the Fae, even to the point of calling others who spoke of fairies and such like as "Fluffy" and "Living in cloud cuckoo land".

I was driving home from work (as a nurse working on a busy unit) not even thinking about anything spiritual, but instead playing the day's events over in my head while trying to concentrate on driving, I turned on the radio for a bit of peace from my busy brain, whilst driving over a small bridge in the village of Chorley in North West Lancashire. The embankment of the river had a train track running along the side of it and the bridge went over the top of them both.

A song I knew was on the radio so I started to sing with the song whilst crossing the bridge when my attention was drawn to something on fire on the pavement. As I drove near I noticed it was a little being completely made up of flame, only about 10 inches long, striding over the bridge in huge strides for something so small. I shook my head in disbelief and looked in my rear view mirror to prove to myself that there was nothing there. To my surprise the small moving fire was still glowing on the path.

I pulled over as soon as it was safe to do so in the next side road to collect my thoughts and to try and process what I had just seen. I could not understand what it was, I was really puzzled.

When I arrived home, I logged onto the internet to research this strange being. I thought it may even have been some sort of alien. I went on a very popular pagan forum and posed the question of what they thought this entity could be and the answers I got back changed my life completely.

The consensus concluded was that I had seen a type of elemental being, a fire sprite which itself is a type of Fae (Faery). After the sighting I started to research the Fae and have taken on attributes of the fire sprite. Even to the point of dressing as one for entertainment purposes whilst fire dancing and providing entertainment for children.

I have trusted in the Fae for the last 3 years and since doing so my life has become better and better. My bipolar hardly affects me now as I fill my life with the joy of the Fae. My life is so full of smiling children, glitter and laughter I do not have time to feel down and when I am hyper I make costumes, paint or write about the Fae.

However, my life did change, my job as a palliative nursing sister was no longer something that I wanted to do (as that put a lot of stress and sadness on my being). I was unclear what I should be doing with my life and what job I should do to pay my way in the world and support my son (as I have been a single parent of 2 boys for all of my adult life). I asked the Fae for guidance and realised what I enjoyed doing the most (dress up, entertain, belly dance and eat fire) was my calling and my character Freyja Fire Sprite has become very popular with children as well as adults! So I started my own business as an entertainer ~ a self-employed Faery. It truly is a magical life.

My advice to everyone reading this book is just go with it, no matter how silly you feel, sillyness is good, it nurtures your inner child and promotes healing to your very core. They say that laughter is the best medicine and that is one thing the Fae love to do! Wisdom is to smile and be free. Be you and don't let anyone live your life for you ~ it's too precious. Have gratitude for what you have, do not be angry or bitter about what you haven't got, fairies in the woods have food, shelter, warmth, family and friends, we don't actually need anything else. To be at one with the Fae, you must work out for yourself what is important and the difference between want and need. Good luck and sparkles!

~ Freyja Fire Sprite (children's entertainer)

Check out www.freyjafiresprite.co.uk to discover more about Freyja's work.

* * *

My first remembered experience with Fairies was when I was 24. My sixth sense had only recently started to open up and it formed the start of my first book Messages from Nature's Guardians, in which I wrote about my experiences of meeting and hearing Nature Spirits and the environmental messages they imparted to me. The first encounter occurred when I was learning to walk outside again after being bedridden for a year unable to move with a serious illness. I remember being aware of energies on the plants and flowers in my parent's garden which was a new experience for me. That was the first time I sensed the Fairies but it was only when I could walk on my own and I went to try and communicate with them that I heard one speak. These were Elemental Fairies and the guardians of plants and flowers. The Fairies told me I was going to teach people about the Elemental world, write books and run courses opening up people's sixth sense so they could learn to communicate with Nature Spirits and Angels too. The Faery world has many dimensions to it and the Elemental Fairies are the easiest to communicate with first I have now discovered. I also work with the Sidhe who are often referred to in folklore as the Gentry or are known as the Magickal Faeries. These Faeries are more human sized and don't have wings like the little friendly Elemental Fairies. They are much more secretive and very much will come into your life when they are calling you rather than the other way around. I met these at a Fairy rathe (mound) near my house in Scotland about 4 years ago. I had walked past it many times but only when I was ready did they show me their magickal energy through my clairsentience (psychic feeling). These Faeries have been guiding me and teaching me about their realm and about how we can work with the Faery Kingdom as well as the other Elemental and Nature Spirit Kingdoms, such as the Elves, Dragons, Unicorns, Gnomes and Mermaids. Some people count these all as Faeries, however they have explained to me that they all have their own races and the Faeries are a unique race in their own right.

The Fairies are constantly helping me in my life if I remember to ask them! I have two personal Guardian Fairies, one is called Romina and one called Eldmina. Romina, who is known as my romance Fairy, helps me with my love life. She guided me to meeting my husband. He ran an environmental company and as I was a former political environmental researcher, he offered me a consultancy post within his company. My other Fairy guide, Eldmina guides me with my spiritual work, so I call upon her regularly in meditation and in rituals. Eldmina guided me along with the Angels to set up my spiritual business, Elemental Beings, to teach people about communicating with the Elemental and Angelic realms.

One time the Fairies really helped me was when we were looking for a new house. We had to be out of the property we were in by a certain date yet had not found anywhere else to live so I sat and wrote a detailed letter to the Fairies stating the kind of property we were looking for, price range, number of bedrooms, even down to specifics such as where I wanted the bathroom to be in the layout and the fact that we didn't want there to be overhead cables going into the house. I folded the letter up, kissed it and placed it on my Fairy alter trusting that the Fairies would guide us to our new home. The weeks passed however and my faith became tested. However, the date we had to be out of the house was getting closer and we still didn't know where we were going to live! So I asked my guardian Fairies where to start looking and I heard them say, "Look the Biggar way!" So the next day I phoned the estate agent in Biggar and described the property we were looking for, the lady who answered said, "We have a property fitting that description but it only became available yesterday, it is not even on the market yet. You would be the first to see it." We visited it the next day and took it on the spot. So we now live in a lovely Fairy house in the country, it has its very own turret too, all thanks to the Fairies' guidance!

As a writer, the Fairies often, along with the other Elementals, guide me on what to write. Sometimes I see them as flashes of twinkling lights or other times they visit me in my dreams and show me what teachings or help they wish to offer us humans at this time. Mostly I hear and feel them around me. Fairies love the creative process and will guide people if they are asked whenever you are being creative. Often they will drop sparks of inspiration into our minds, particularly I find if I am suffering writer's block!

The Fairies are around us all the time just waiting to be asked and invited into our lives. They have to respect our free will on this planet but will often give you signs or clues that they are around even if you are not consciously aware of them. They are passionate about protecting the environment which is their home and get upset when we are disrespectful to the planet. If you are asking them for help and guidance in your life, they will freely help you but they appreciate and bestow more gifts upon you if you help them in their mission too, for example picking up litter, feeding the birds in winter, being kind to animals and not spraying weed killer and other toxic chemicals in your gardens, as well as eating organic food and generally being environmentally aware. The Fairies are good friends to have in your life and the more you communicate with them, the more you will notice them around you!

~ Alphedia (Fiona Murray), Author of *Messages from Nature's Guardians* and *Ascending with Unicorns*.

Visit www.elementalbeings.co.uk for more information on Fiona's work.

Difficult Emotions

Emotion is the most important indicator of your vibrational health. Your vibrational state is best when it is balanced and harmonious. We know we have achieved this when, yes you guessed it, we feel balanced and harmonious. I like to refer to this state as solid. You are not wibbly-wobbling all over the place, or fading in and out like a dodgy radio signal. But life has a habit of happening doesn't it. We will experience the unwanted and these interruptions when computed can throw our emotions into chaos.

Chaos is not bad. You are assimilating some bad event or experience you didn't welcome or plan for! You will eventually reach a settling point again. If you view it like a still river-bed being disturbed by a duck's busy beak. The mud flies every-where but always settles again. Maybe not in the same place, sometimes the river-bed's surface looks significantly different. Yet it remains the same river-bed.

Some emotions speed us up, like rage and jealousy. Some slow us down, like sadness and hopelessness. Check out the charts below, where do you fit at this moment? Where do you want to be?

Faerie states of being

Light, peaceful, harmony, connected, capable, strong, resilient, happy, loving, calm, joyful, excited, positive, awake, energised, generous, acceptance, gratitude, limitless.

Non-faerie states of being

Heavy, chaotic, discord, disconnected, incapable, weak, wobbly, sad, frightened, anxious, joyless, panic, negative, numb, exhausted, jealous, resistance, poverty, limited.

What do you notice about these lists? Yes, they are almost opposites. For a faerie state there is a non-faerie state. So in other words, yes you got it ~ emotions are on a vibrational spectrum. If you have an emotional state right now, you can move along the spectrum. Note I say move ~ not jumping nor climbing.

No climbing!

We do not 'progress' through stages of emotion. No one is further on, or higher up. We are all feeling beings, vulnerable to our emotions changing to reflect how we perceive events.

Definitely no jumping in the shallow end!

The emotional vibrational spectrum is to be swam up, not jumped in. What do I mean? Well, many people on hearing that emotions are a spectrum, for e.g. love on one end, fear on the other, will try to jump to love when they live in fear. This is a big vibrational ask! Often it is a form of self-sabotage to jump the spectrum. The idea is to feel relieved that emotions are on a spectrum and then to move across the spectrum to find lasting relief.

Moving across the spectrum

Sit quietly and define where you are on the spectrum. Accept where you are. You will want to deny it but stay with it and ask yourself these questions:

What is the better feeling closest to your current state?
What would it take to get you there?
Are you willing to let go to get there?
Can you forgive yourself for feeling as you do?

Forgive yourself for feeling something other than what is wanted.

Living is feeling. If you stop feeling the contrast between emotions, you have stopped having preferences. This is the realm of expansion and creation ~ desire depends upon preference and espouses creation. Creation needs you to choose one thing over another.

Why it's good to feel

We have been encouraged to believe that there is a proper way to manoeuvre our way through the world and that is by thinking. It is not surprising that thinking is seen as the male aspect and feeling the feminine. Look at what our non-feeling selves have created. Look at the world with its absent goddess, wow does she need to awaken from her oppressed coma. Unless we become a feeling sepsis we will continue to mess up. Unless we stop fearing being led astray by our feelings the mind will continue to lead us astray. Emotion is not to be feared, emotion is extremely transient. How we perceive the feeling is the real doozy. How we dress our feelings in meaning, blame, reasons, morality and so on is what complicates and submerges the feeling into the realms of the shadow self. Emotions are not rocks they are rivers, they are fluid. Emotions are massive sign posts on your path telling you where you are and how many miles it is to peace of mind. Every single 'negative' emotion has been on your side steering you towards your own happiness. Like a really good navigator the negative shouts loudly and clearly that you are off course! Fear is showing you love.

Discussing discord with others

They will either disagree or agree and both are terrible for you. If you need to talk discuss with someone objective who will not cement you in the feeling and toss you in a river. Seriously, discuss with someone who will encourage you to look at the pattern and let the pattern go, not help you grab the pattern and solidify it as your personality. A good counsellor, spiritual coach, or your friends at the Faerie Ring are all good objective places to start.

Ritual for overcoming difficult emotions

A lot of the activities in this book are designed to connect you with your creativity. Many may appear childish, light-hearted and silly and indeed they are! They are meant to be as it is within the heart of a child that our creativity resides. However, I'm not presuming for one minute you like connecting with your childish self. In fact, for many of you childhood is a landscape you want to pave over and forget. Chipping the childhood asphalt can feel really threatening. You may inexplicably find you are remembering events or feeling emotions that hurt or trouble you. If these feelings become overwhelming please consult a counsellor or trusted healer. For most of you the following ritual will be enough to integrate, channel and manage your difficult emotions in a helpful, fruitful and creative way.

Go to your sacred place (or if away from home find a quiet place). Light a candle. Listen to your breath ~ don't try to change its depth, rhythm or flow. Let your breathing lead you, trust its song. Move to noticing what you feel. Where is the feeling? What shape is it? What colour? What speed? Take the shape and move it from your body out into the space in front of you. Notice the emotion's colour, its speed, its form as it moves in front of you. Now ask the feeling these questions. Wait for an answer before moving from one question to another.

What are you trying to protect me from?

What can I do to help you?

How can we work together to protect me in a more productive way? (notice the shape change colour, speed and form)

Once the emotion has changed shape, colour and speed breathe it back into your heart. Sit for a while. Now take your paper and state clearly:

Any residual, unnecessary, unproductive, wasteful binds, bonds, vows, attachments, hooks or punishments I breathe out into this friendly tree for transmutation.

Breathe deeply onto the paper. Any ideas, conclusions, emotions or inspirations that come up write them down on the paper. Fold your paper. Light one end in the candle's flame and throw into the head proof dish and watch it fizzle and burn away.

State "All is light, all is love. I am that I AM. And all returns to the centre which is love."

Listen to your breathing again. Feel how you feel. Enjoy the sensation within you. Write your discoveries in your faerie journal. Remember you are loved. I and the faeries send you love and wherever you are I'm sending you a cosmic cuddle.

About Me

My prayer to myself:

For each breath
For each heart beat
For each inspired word
For each moment of connection ~ I thank you

This section of the book has been the hardest to write. I have danced away from being here, sat in front of my laptop, about to show you parts of myself and my life that usually stay hidden. I've been calling it writer's block, as if that explains something. Yet as every writer knows, writer's block is simply fear of telling the truth.

Childhood

As a child I was a climber. I liked climbing trees, walls, roofs ~ anything my gangly legs could scramble up. There were plenty of walls in Gorton, Manchester. Rows and rows of terraced houses felt my feet scamper across them. I liked sitting with the tom cats watching the stars. Climbing was supreme. I simultaneously felt strong, impressive and free. I was a quiet, odd, socially awkward child. My sisters were the two people I would talk or fight with but apart from them I was a loner.

I hated school with a silent rage. I was confused by the rules and angry with my teachers for taking me away from play. My dyscalculia and dyslexia didn't help and it didn't take me long to view myself as chronically stupid and incapable.

I can remember hunger too. Hunger like nothing I've experienced since. We had no food, no heating, no bedclothes, no carpets. Home was bleak ~ mostly due to my father's silence (I've never once had a conversation with him) and the oppressive way he treated my mother saw her eventually turn to drink. Watching my mother, a vibrant creative artist lose herself to alcoholism remains the saddest experience of my life. My mother lost both her parents in her teens and met my Irish catholic soldier father when she was eighteen. They came to England, married and had my elder sister. Then twins, my sister and I. Love was hard for my mother. She had lost people which seemed to leave her feeling unsafe to offer love, in case her love would kill. Her grief isolated her in an angry bubble ~ she often seemed so fragile and sad. I felt guilty for needing things from her that she didn't have the emotional range to give.

Looking back with adult's eyes it is easy to say I was lonely and afraid as a child but that's not all I was. There were happy times. They were often spent inside my imagination, which I grew to rely on. Imagination's ability to bend time and make darkness bright is something I believe in and see work for adult survivors time and time again.

Stories

I would sit in the airing cupboard (my time machine) for hours visiting everywhere and anywhere I wanted, or my twin sister Theresa requested (usually the Bermuda triangle for some reason) and then I would retell her of my adventures until she shoved me back in to invent some more. She was totally convinced I disappeared once the door was shut and despite it seeming like a practical joke, it wasn't. We needed the release only imagination can bring. We both needed to believe. It was around this time my mother invented Whilimeana in Wellies. A long legged faerie that she drew dancing on teacups and swimming in puddles, 'Whilimeana' she told me 'lives in the skirting board. Behind them is her world'. I was convinced and began to leave her letters crammed into every nook and cranny of the house. Somehow it never bothered me that she didn't write back. Yet even now she appears in my dreams to offer me wellies, umbrellas and occasionally a hug.

I also had a collection of small fashion dolls. I cut their hair; felt-tipped their faces and invented a whole new world. It made my sisters laugh and whatever was occurring elsewhere disappeared. Stories became vitally important to me around this time. Symbols and metaphor offered me a safe distance from myself and my experience. It helped me process my confusion ~ it's extremely difficult processing neglect as a child. I loved my parents immensely. It took me a long time to realise their abusive co-dependant relationship had very little to do with us as children. It was about them. Although I blamed myself for their unhappiness, disappointment and anger for many years, I learnt to understand them as people, not parents, and it helped.

Adolescence

As a teenager I had a great big black-hole where my self-esteem should have been. My rage had increased and I spent less and less time at home even if it meant sleeping rough. I no longer wanted to speak with my sisters and had no friends only familiars who didn't want to go home either. I walked the corridors of secondary school like a cyborg ~ jaw set and radiating 'fuck off.' By fourteen I was drinking daily and no longer in school. I wanted a way out of my life and couldn't see one. I needed money to drink so trawled local cafés looking for work and found a small restaurant that offered me a cleaning position on Saturday mornings. Determined to make it work, I arrived early. For the life of me I cannot remember his name. I remember he owned the place, I remember he led me down into the cellar and I remember he raped me. I remember very calmly talking him out of killing us both. And very very clearly I remember feeling sorry for him. He babbled about his ill wife, his shame, his god. Despite my bruises and fear, I felt I'd done something awful to him. He eventually let me free and never before, or since, have I felt so grateful to another person. If you haven't experienced being held against your will you probably think my reaction is odd or unusual. It's not. Telling my mother was the hardest thing I've ever done, but she wasn't resilient enough to hear, she blamed me.

Silent, I climbed into bed; dreamt of elephants and woke with a fever. Days I stayed there; listening to my sisters moving around, burning internally, bleeding. Sometimes one of my sisters would pop their heads in and ask if I was okay. Their love hurt. I stayed silent. I would dream it all away. For many years I did.

Weeks later I heard he'd killed himself. I was in the corner shop and they were discussing him, his family and his dying wife. I wondered what dying felt like. I began to obsess trying to imagine the sensation of actually dying. Years later, I would walk past a murder scene in Hulme decorated with flowers and the imagined sensations would flood me and become a short story that would eventually become my stage play 'Seconds'.

Home became unbearable. I began hanging around the streets. Sometimes the streets feel safer. Sometimes sleeping in bushes is preferable. I felt nothing. I was numb inside like someone had switched off my humanity. I met petty criminals. We stole cars and drank till we dropped. At fourteen I had lived enough and wanted out ~ I didn't care how. My self-hatred was palpable.

I was raped for a second time just before my fifteenth birthday. My sister and I were at a party. I had gone to get my coat when he grabbed me and forced me into a room. My rage was brilliant and fierce; I fought, kicking and punching, but to no avail. My body was simply too weak. My sister and I ran home ~ me terrified he might be following us and kill her like he said. We held hands and ran like horses ~ just like we did when we were little. Sometimes when we were small, we'd be winged unicorns, but that night we felt too heavy to take flight.

Not long after this, I met my husband. He too was a drinker like me. He was also silent and it took me ten years to realise I had married my father. We broke up not long after my first play was produced. After being with him just a few months, my parents left and went home to Ireland. My sisters and I were left with the choice to go with them, or stay in England. My eldest sister was sitting her A-Levels and moved in with her then boyfriend, my twin sister had nowhere to go and opted for Ireland. I had just found out I was pregnant, so moved in with my soon to be husband's family. I stopped drinking and smoking. At the ripe old age of seventeen I gave birth to my beautiful magnificent daughter Emmy. Three days later I died due to a medical error. Someone forgot to give me a blood transfusion; slowly in my own unique silent way I disintegrated unnoticed and without complaint.

My death experience

It is true that you see a white light. But I had no tunnel and no one met me. Whilimeana was there, her wings glittering in my peripheral vision. I was simply floating in white light ~ tranquil, peaceful and so so warm was the sensation of love that when I returned I cried on and off for days.

Motherhood

Due to a superbug, it took me close to a year to be fully back on my feet. During this time my husband ran up huge debts and we lost our home after only two years of living there. I moved into a small place in Bolton to be near my twin sister. Days later I fell ill with scarlet fever and lay for days unable to move. It was Christmas and Emmy was eating cereal out of the box and snuggling me for warmth. We watched the Lion King over and over. It was a desperately unhappy time. I was chronically lonely and felt powerless to change any aspect of my life. Event after event appeared to be happening to me. People and situations seemed to invade my life without my knowledge or consent.

Once I regained my strength, Emmy and I would walk for

miles in the snow that winter. Our favourite place was the icy river ~ she loved the natural world and was insatiable. I joined a library and read up on birds, mammals and fish so I could answer her questions. I made up stories that made her laugh. I clung to her smile in a desperate attempt to avoid the dead feeling inside. She helped me feel alive and it was painful. I came to realise the pain was vibrant to remind me I cared about my life. That I wanted my life to be different ~ I just didn't know how to change it.

My husband found a house near to where he worked in Cheshire. Soon Emmy and I joined him there. Around two weeks into living there I had a full emotional breakdown, of which I remember very little. I remember lying on my kitchen floor and feeling as if my chest were literally caving in, like air was passing through me and pulling my chest inside out. My sense of self fragmented. It took the love of many people, including myself, to put me back together again. I was twenty years old.

Over the next five years I entered into intensive psychotherapy, counselling and support groups. I discovered my voice. I had energy healing, shamanic counselling and soul retrieval. We took our first family holiday to Wales, we had little money and I was very ill. My body had little resilience and I often slept for hours after walking just a few miles. Yet my daughter's infallible ability to be inside every moment pulled me forward ~ we collected shells and searched for crabs. I remembered I could be happy. I stood by the sea and felt an overwhelming desire to sing ~ I did. Emmy and I stood there and sang out to the horizon. Something new was occurring.

The next day I bought a beach book. Perhaps one of the worst books I've ever read! I am forever indebted to the author, for in that book I remembered me. Something close to ambition, but more resembling desire, rekindled within me. I'm going to write a book I said, which is no mean feat for a dyslexic. And I went on to do just that.

Awakening my faerie-self

My novel was a good story but badly written. Every morning I would get up at 5am to write by hand – scribble, scribble, scribble. Creating felt so wonderful. I sent my novel to people all over the world and they unanimously hated it and I didn't care. I grabbed their feedback and wrote another book. I entered this one in Commonword's annual competition to find the north of England's best new novelist ~ and I came runner up! Riding on the encouragement I went to college. Entering education again was a huge deal ~ I decided on counselling. I loved Carl Rogers' theories, they had helped to heal me and I wanted to heal the world. I volunteered with victims of crime and teenage mothers. Those four years were magnificent. I even went to the theatre for the first time at 29 and decided to write my first play 'The Crucifixion of Madeline Mackay'. I dared to send it away and to my surprise it was produced for a little festival in London. The play was a hard one to watch being about my experiences as a rape survivor. Around this time, I started to work with and meet other creative women, watch my daughter grow into an expressive artist in her own right and I felt strong. I discovered the power of reconnecting with your elemental self, the wild child, the changeling, the silly dancing pagan poet. I began to dream about Whilimeana. Why, I would think on waking and then it became apparent.

Prediction magazine and 6th Books

The 6th Books publishing competition appeared in Prediction magazine. At the time I was preparing for my second play 'Seconds' to be performed at the Pleasance in London. I had little time to put into a big writing project so thought about how good it would be to enter but didn't. Yet every night my dreams would fill with glitter and faerie wings. Every morning I would awaken feeling pulled to submit my ideas. For they are just my ideas ~ they are simply the things I did and others did and you have just done to rekindle your magic, to get passion burning again, to awaken the inner faerie. I guess it was my time as the book is in your hands. I hope it helps you in whatever way it can.

So yes this journey has been a tough one. It has been dark, but I have found some nuggets of gold and silver along the way. A little bit of knowledge I wanted to share with you. In my sharing, I have learnt even more about myself. I have become an activist, street artist and work with women seekers daily. Wee are all in the process of awakening the sleeping goddess and we need each other more than ever. We need to tell each other our stories. Honour each others' experiences and journeys. We need to support and enable each other to unchain the imprisoned goddess. Lastly, I want to say that it has been a lovely, enjoyable and expanding experience spending this time with you. Thank you for reading, thank you for being here and please, keep in touch.

Alex (River) Clarke

Faerie friendly links

Come and join our Faerie Community on Facebook!
www.facebook.com/pages/The-Faerie-Ring

Keep up to date with my projects by following me on Twitter @AlexClarkes The brilliant Prediction Magazine
www.predictionmagazine.co.uk

For free downloadable Mandalas:
www.mandalaproject.org

To insightful FAE articles and competitions:
www.faemagazine.com

For healing and wellbeing:
www.lightofhope.co.uk

For party entertainment:
www.freyjafiresprite.co.uk

For life coaching:
www.celestiallifecoaching.wordpress.com

For shamanic drumming:
www.shamanicdrumming.com/free_downloads.html

For women's drumming tuition try:
www.facebook.com/pages/Wangari/ or
www.kontaani.net/workshopseventsandperformances.cfm

BOOKS

6th Books investigates the paranormal, supernatural, explainable or unexplainable. Titles cover everything included within parapsychology: how to, lifestyles, beliefs, myths, theories and memoir.